Designing the American Home for Market Value

Designing the American Home for Market Value

Don't Remodel or Build Your House
Until You Read This Book

BOB RHODY

Redwood Publishing, LLC

Printed in the United States of America

First Printing, 2020
ISBN 978-1-7344254-7-5 (paperback)
ISBN 978-1-7344254-8-2 (ebook)

Library of Congress Cataloguing Number: 2020907538

Published by Redwood Publishing, LLC
Orange County, California
www.redwooddigitalpublishing.com

To contact the author, please write to Bob Rhody at *brhody@earthlink.net*

10 9 8 7 6 5 4 3 2 1

Foreword

If you are not a contractor or an experienced homebuilder or developer, remodeling a home can keep you up all night. Any of these thoughts have or will occur to you in the days and weeks, months and years to come as you go through this process:

- Putting in gutters can kill you.
- Building a swimming pool more than four feet deep can kill others.
- Putting in a vaulted gable ceiling in a sleeping area may lead you to soon go under the knife.
- The wrong swing of exterior doors are inviting to burglars.
- Stairs can lead to broken bones or it can kill you.
- Saunas or spas can kill you.
- Rats will find their way in.
- Solar will lead you to the poor house.
- Trees will burn down your house.

- Lack of planning can lead to divorce.
- Five second motion lights can save your life.

Alarming? Positively! That is why you must read this "Bible" of home remodeling!

What This Book Does Not Include:

- This book does not include kitchen layout or decorations. It does, however, include the proper position of the kitchen in the house.
- It does not include how to do plumbing, electrical, or carpentry. It does, however, cover where to place them.
- It does not include landscape species of plants and the various varieties. It does, however, cover location.
- It does not include how to sell your house or how to build it. It does, however, cover how to get the best return on your investment.
- It does not include interior design or decorations. Instead, it will show you how to utilize every square foot of your house.
- It does not include places and persons for your project, but it will suggest how to find them.
- When I don't know something, I call an expert. In this case, I'm sharing my expertise to give you powerful insight into building the house of your dreams.

Proven Results

Everything in this book has been proven correct over a long period of time. These are not suggestions; each decision you make will impact you in some way and affect your life going forward. Should you have any comments as you read this book, feel free to email the author, Bob Rhody at: *brhody@earthlink.net* and he will respond as time permits.

As you read through many other how-to books, especially those with illustrations and pictures, you will find, perhaps, a few items to help you. **But in this book, you will find help on every page.** It is guaranteed to be extraordinary!

So listen to sound advice. There is nothing more comforting than to live in a well-designed house. I hope you enjoy the knowledge—it has taken years to acquire.

Use it well!

Bob Rhody

About the Author

Bob Rhody has served as a project designer for many years, including an extensive amount of time in new developments seeing the good, the bad, and the ugly. And that is why this book was written.

Chances are, you don't have the luxury of time before beginning your project. This is why I would encourage you to review every chapter and every word, then make notes—lots of notes.

Even today, Bob spends most Sundays devoted to home tours where he visits everything from small, everyday homes, to large, expensive custom-built homes that are for sale. At these open houses, there is always a Realtor or agent greeting people near the entrance, welcoming the visitor. After touring the house and seeing what he considers poor design, the author usually will engage the agent, stating his professional opinion. In the process of *opening the door* to casual conversation, the agent will often open up and say, "Yes, this item has been mentioned by other potential buyers."

There are two types of wrong design possible on the buyer's mind:

- The first is the obvious: Why do you have the dining room table with seating for twelve next to an island with seating for eight?
- The second is the design flaw where a buyer says, "I don't like this but I don't know why."

This may be because all of the kitchen wall cabinets have glass doors, the island has no seating or there is no island at all. They may see the master bath with the washbasins so close together that there is little counter space, or the foot of the bed faces the entry door of the bedroom.

Don't worry—every major item of good or bad design will be covered in this book, which many consider the "Bible" of how to remodel or build your house. What you absolutely don't want is design and amenities that will place your home below market value. We all have limited time on this planet so let's live life to its fullest.

Cyrus said to shoot for the moon. If you miss, you will be among the stars.

Fast Guide to Reading

Table of Contents

1

Getting Started

The Middle Class
Budget
Definitions and Designations

Getting Started

THE MIDDLE CLASS

This book is meant to assist you, the middle-class homeowner, to properly remodel or build your house. Historically, the first true gathering of the middle class was living in suburban track houses.

During the time of the formation of the thirteen colonies, 75% of homeowners in the country were middle class. This left 5% for the upper class and 20% for the lower class, such as slaves and immigrants coming to this country to do the meager tasks, construction work, and farming.

Today, the middle class is at 78% and is made up of the descendants of slaves, immigrants with special skills, like engineers from Asia, and the huge group of Americans who, wanting to improve their lives, gambled on capitalism (this gambling is not the same as a casino player).

The question is, in this country, does the average citizen have a chance to get lucky? The answer *is* yes, but with a gamble. That is why the banking segment has risen to spectacular heights. They made it by making loans to gamblers, those who gambled on a better life.

You are a gambler. You gamble on the task of remodeling with the anticipation that your project will be a winner. You complete the work and it *IS* work. In the middle of the night, you walk into your new kitchen, turn on the lights, and marvel at what you have accomplished. Your kitchen glows. You have become the winner.

In a casino you have less than a 50% chance to win. In capitalistic America, you have a better than 50% chance to do well. But this is not laying down a bet; it is by working very hard at the tasks ahead. The harder you work, the better chance you have at winning. Winning in this environment means making life better for you and your family.

The main reason America is the world's leader is augmented by working women. A majority of homeowners who qualify for a home purchase are due to their combined income. This shines a light on the consistency of the middle class.

Education plays a big role, as we know. The better educated, the better the job, and therefore, more income. Much is maligned about our country's education system but it works and works very well.

When attending a university and doing well (or not), a student's mind is put to the options that education provides. This is ingrained in every student as they envision the possibilities of a better life. A student can attend only one class on only one day, but still want to become the next Frank Lloyd Wright or Abraham Lincoln.

Today, 6% of the American population is considered upper class. Yesterday's millionaires are today's billionaires. This is a small group, but they control 80% of the stock market. Many of these billionaires were once part of the middle class, and a small percentage, of the lower class.

One hundred years from now, that 6% will not change much. Only one can win the mega jackpot lottery. (Time to buy a ticket?) Talk about being lucky. This leaves 14% lower class. Seems like a small number, but it is huge. The reason is unskilled migrants. So you think immigrants entering this country is a problem? Nearly every person entering in the 16th century were immigrants.

This author's grandfather came to this country from Germany in 1915 with nothing but the shirt on his back. Today, his family owns 6,000 acres of cotton fields in Texas. If they were to subdivide that land into middle class homes, then 30,000 homes could be built. The door is always open.

As a middle class homeowner, you may not want to strive for 6,000 acres of land, but you want your house on your lot to be spectacular. This is the point of this book. You may have heard the term "keeping up with the Joneses." The author submits to you—you are the Joneses.

America is a Land of Builders

There are a few designers who believe the design layout of a house is subjective. It is not. Good design is directly related to value. Value is what you can get for your house once it's sold. You may not be remodeling your house right now to sell, but one day it will sell, and the better the design with which you do it, the more money it will return.

There are plenty of examples of what constitutes good or bad design. Just go to any model home or planned community in America. There, you most likely will see a good layout which should tell you these large developers of tract homes have done the research to design houses that will sell. You should do the same. Be astute and don't try to change the formula. You can't expect different results by changing a formula that has been used over and over with successful results.

You may have to drive a long distance, perhaps to another city to see model homes. But go anyway. You will be glad you did. You may want to consider staying at an inn, motel, hotel, or Airbnb so you can spend the time you need and do your due diligence. Make a weekend of it—drive there on a Saturday so you can be at the Sunday opening, which is generally at 10 a.m. While you're there, ask about other developments nearby. You can never see too much.

This author once took his daughter to see such a development for the purpose of writing this book. Much to my surprise, she ended up purchasing a home there! Good design is directly related to the value it produces.

When you go, be sure to take a camera or use your cell phone to take pictures because you will not remember everything you see. Sales people will give you a layout and pictures of their model homes. Study and compare those with what you read in this book.

Begin with the end in mind—that is, your preliminary plan must have *resale* in mind. Compare it to what you feel you want. It's your house and you're going to have to live in it. If you aren't making good decisions at this point, you may regret it later.

Most homeowners do not start this way. They see other projects in the neighborhood and take bits and pieces of each and then try to fit them together. Wrong! Just because it looks nice in someone else's home, doesn't mean it will work in yours.

Good Design is Directly Related to the Value it Produces

The basic layout of a house today is not the same as mid-century design or any other time in history.

The first preliminary plan should show all the rooms drawn to scale (more about this later). Start with the location of primary rooms: first is the master bedroom which is the largest bedroom. It should face the rear of the house or the backyard. Also facing the rear of the house are the master bath, family room, kitchen and breakfast room. All other rooms can face the rear, as well, but when space is limited, the primary rooms should be placed there first. Those rooms that are not primary can face the front or the sides.

Facing the front of the house are the entry, living room (if you choose to have one), dining room, and all other rooms, including bedrooms, small guest suite, and office, if you have one. The laundry room can face the side with a window. The breakfast room can also face the side. Try to have a window in all baths, except the powder room. Windows are not necessary in the closet, wardrobe, hall, stairwell, or pantry, but the garage is optional.

This author will not give you the opinion of options too often. What is not an option is to do it correctly without exception. How would you like me living with you making all of these decisions...? I thought so!

If it is not possible to put primary rooms facing the rear, then limit it to these three rooms: the master bedroom, master bath, and family room. The kitchen should be part of the family room (more later) and can face the rear but not necessarily against the rear wall. It could have a sink and an island but from the sink, you must face the rear yard looking through the family room with a clear view outside to the pool, if you have one.

Why do this? The main reason is to watch the children as they play in the yard or by the pool from a standing location where you spend most of your time, and you spend the majority of your time in primary rooms. The other reason is to see your guests and pets. Many buyers don't realize this is important. They only know it when they see it. If they buy a house without proper location of its rooms, they will grow to regret their purchase.

Don't take a chance, do it right. Do you want your dream house to come true, or do you want to cry a river?

Is Your Floor Plan Stale?

Next is to determine the size of rooms. The master bedroom should be, at minimum, 20% larger than the secondary bedroom, and the other bedrooms should be at least 10% smaller than the secondary. It's okay to have bedroom #3 and bedroom #4 the same size. The family room should be the largest room in the house to accommodate at least a sofa or sectional, two chairs, and a coffee table.

The master bedroom should be large enough to accommodate at least a king size bed and two night stands. A walk-in closet is a must. If you don't have a lot of room, put in a smaller walk-in closet. Good planning is everything. (I don't recommend mirrors but we'll talk about that later.)

The master bath should have a separate tub and shower. Size matters less than the need for both units. Smaller tub, smaller shower? No problem. You now have the ingredients of a true master bath.

With today's open kitchen needs, the kitchen should have a view of the entire family room and have an island. No island? Bad choice! The kitchen should have ample wall space to accommodate a television.

It's so nice to hear family and friends tell about the great experience they had remodeling their house. Don't be taken in by their enthusiasm. Most likely, they haven't reached the shock syndrome. That comes later—way later.

Once again, the value of a basic plan is what you can get for your house once sold. You may have heard of "loan to value." This is a term used by finance companies to determine what the maximum amount of money is that can be loaned on your property. It is market value of your house, divided by the dollar amount the financial institution will loan, i.e., a market value of $500,000 divided by what will be a loan of perhaps $250,000. The loan value will be 50%.

The objective is to get, for your house, the highest market value and the best possible loan. But you say you are not selling your house, you are remodeling. When does loan to value come into play for you? It's the money you will get once you sell. ALL HOMES SELL sooner or later. You need to be on guard. Your house WILL SELL SOMETIME.

Home is Your Happy Place

Are you in a quandary? You need not be. In this book, you will learn what to do. If you stop reading here, you may be sorry. Which leads us back to the meaning of basic design.

Now that you know that *basics* is the foundation of our society and of our daily lives. Most people shower in the morning, have coffee shortly after, and put gas in their car. Positioning rooms on your floor plan properly is doing the basics that you cannot ignore. The basics are a win-win proposition.

First and foremost, you must get above the billowing cloud. Your neighbor added a dining room without a window, your aunt Elsie built a master bath without a tub, your uncle Joe added the main staircase at the rear of the house, and your sister did a kitchen island without seating. All this and more goes against the basics of good design. It may have been what they wanted when sugar in their coffee proved to be salt. It's not what they wanted, it is what they should have done.

Common response: "I've put all this money into my house. Why can't I get it back?"

Answer: Were the basics followed? No, not in the least.

Let's discuss the basics. Basic in design and basics in other fields are compatible. John Wooden, the late coach of the UCLA basketball team, was asked, prior to the UCLA North Carolina championship game in 1974, "What is your game plan?"

His answer prior to the game was, "We will stick to the basics."

Question: What do you think of the other team? His answer: "Makes no difference who we play. We will play basic basketball. If we do our job right, we will win."

Under John Wooden's guidance, UCLA went on to beat North Carolina and seal Coach Wooden's 10th National Championship, which no coach has done in fifty years. He became the only coach in college basketball history to win ten National Championships in a span of sixteen years.

Can you believe that not one of thousands of coaches would adopt John Wooden's philosophy of basic game-winning basketball? But you can! Stick to the basics.

Or, as an alternative, you'll stand in front of your house and wonder why you did not get the price you wanted and you'll cry. Don't let this happen. Be proactive. Maybe your children will sell the house as an inheritance. Do you want them doing the crying?

Getting the Returns You Want

First you must itemize a list of costs. Start with the last thing first: the appliances. Begin by going to the appliance store to see the latest appliances that are available. You will be pleasantly surprised at what is out there.

Ask the salesperson to help. Tell them you are putting together a budget and would like to know what is new, on sale, and available. Later, you can shop for the best price, but today you want to see and touch.

There, you may find a six foot refrigerator or a sink/dishwasher combination only 34" wide. Choose what you like and request the list in writing with dimensions. These exact items may not be what you will use and adjustments will have to be made.

This is good for a second reason. As you proceed with the planning/budget you will talk to others and see different appliance options, which, of course, will change the budget. That's okay. You are working the process. Anything you do, do it well. The last thing you want is to be sorry for what you didn't do.

Next are plumbing items. Okay, why you ask, are we not starting with construction costs? Because we are working on a true budget. Appliances can vary from a cook top to a freestanding range, but plumbing fixtures are relatively fixed. You need one toilet for each bath. Fixed.

Again, go to a plumbing fixtures showroom to see, not only what is available, but what meets your expectations. This is the time to stop and compare. Do you want standard items or high end? Let's categorize "standard" as items that will fit the purpose. Today's fixtures come under the "green" requirements (more about green later). Whether the toilet is $59 or $590, it must meet green energy standards. But don't concern yourself with this. All that you can purchase today are energy efficient, unless you buy in Mexico.

That's not a joke. Foreign countries still produce non-efficient, non-conforming items.

This author firmly believes that if other countries would insist on proper construction items, the countries would be able to move away from third-world status and advance themselves. Enough about politics.

At this point, you may not know if your plan will be to add a spa tub/shower or a shower only. The objective now is to see what the various costs are in order to start your budget. Put together a chart.

The football team entered the field without a place kicker. Oops! The objective of getting a hold on costs of appliances and plumbing fixtures is to see what you have left in your budget. Bring life to your floor plan.

Fall into the Realm of Common Sense

Now that you have a rough idea about costs of appliances and plumbing fixtures, you can move onto the next list of required items: architecture, engineering, and permit fees. Start with the last item first. Go to the department issuing permits to ask what the plan check fees and permit fees are? You will need to give them the evaluation, not details. They will give you a plan check fee amount and a permit fee amount. The total of these fees are part of your budget.

While it may vary after plans are drawn, you are now only looking for a budget. Anticipate a larger fee at the end. That always happens. This is the real world!

You are taking baby steps. You have three items helping you on a yet determined final budget. Next, check with an architect (see section: Finding an Architect). You want to know their fees and what is provided. You want a preliminary plan drawn first for a separate fee. A preliminary plan is the existing floor plan plus, to include tear out (demolition), plus the proposed work.

Questions to the architect:

1. Will plans show what you want?
2. Ideas and comments.
3. Cost of changes.
4. Cost of printing plans. (Who pays for printing?)

Now you are done with the preliminary plan. What to do next? Call a contractor—someone who will sit down and discuss the overall project with you. Show the contractor your appliance and plumbing quotes. This is the time to determine if the envisioned project can come to fruition before investing in complete plans.

All this is good and worth consideration. Hammer straight! Put the edge in "educate."

BUDGET

What is the Cost at the Moment?

Your next major endeavor is the budget. In order to come up with an accurate budget, you must fit everything into it. To put it this way, you would not go out with only one sock and one shoe.

With the preliminary floor plan, the cost of remodeling can be determined by asking a local real estate agent to appraise your house. Choose an established Realtor with a history of multiple sales in your area. Generally, a Realtor will be accommodating with the thought that they might get a listing in the near future. When you do sell, strongly consider this helpful Realtor.

Next, after showing the Realtor your floor plan, ask if you can see a house close to your expectations, finished as close as possible to your new plans. This house or houses' sale price, or expected sale price, will give you a close comparison of what to expect—better than 85% accurate.

Deduct your appraised value from the house or houses completed that are, or will be, for sale. This is your expected starting budget. This is the amount of money you need to meet your goal. If the amount is too high, then you should reduce your plans to meet your financial capability.

Generally, your budget to do this remodel will be within your reach. You would not have started this process unless you had money close at hand. Consider financing if you do not have the cash. Take your package to the bank providing the lowest interest. Unfortunately, the banks do not care about plans; they are looking at your credit score and ability to pay back the loan. Wow, the proposed plan appraisal of your house, as it stands now, and the comparison house are worlds apart.

Until you have the cash in hand or promised, don't hire an architect. You may want to adjust these plans to fit your budget and your financial capabilities. If you hire an architect and you don't have the cash to do the work, then your dream may never get off the ground. Unfortunately, this is the case 40% of the time. Ask any architect.

A home equity line of credit is a good way to go. Don't refinance at this stage since it's possible the money derived could come up short and you won't be able to complete your project. If you are short, then credit cards might be the answer. However, they will cost a high interest rate. Once you have a loan approved, it will be easier to pay off credit cards for your project at a later date.

Cut Corners vs. Invest More

Only after the project is completed should you refinance because you will have increased your property value. Use the money from the refinance to pay off your credit cards. The interest should then be factored into the overall budget. Make it an exact science. Do it right, and at the end you can say to yourself, "Job well done."

Now with financing in place but not consummated, it's time to choose an architect to draw only the preliminary plan to get quotes, in order to form a realistic budget. The building department will accept a licensed or an unlicensed architect. They will also accept plans drawn by you, though it's not a good idea to draw your own plans.

Instead, draw up ideas that you have for your architect to incorporate into the final plans. Research drafting services. You may save money at this early stage. Before you go to an architect, make a wish list of what you desire. This should consist of the following:

1. Cabinet style: shaker, custom, or sleek.
2. Counter top materials.
3. Hanging light fixtures: recessed or sconces.
4. Pantry and closet interiors.
5. Doors: molding style and crown molding.
6. Door hardware color and type.
7. Appliances: oven, cook top, freestanding range, refrigerator, microwave (check out the drawer microwave), and disposers.
8. Tile: wall, floor, shower walls and floor, and kitchen backsplash.
9. Shower doors: consider frameless—cost more but looks great and is easier to keep clean.
10. Painting interior and exterior (always paint after all work is done).
11. Plumbing fixtures: sinks, toilets, faucets and valves, tubs, air switch for disposer.
12. Low voltage: TV, internet, security and speakers.
13. Revised budget.
14. Roofing: tile or shingles.
15. Floor covering: composite, tile, cork or carpet, or natural oak or maplewood.

Budget—Save vs. Where to Invest More

After the preliminary plan is drawn and you have at least one reliable quote, it's time to revise the budget. The preliminary plan should be your ultimate wish list. If it is too costly, then make revisions by lowering your expectations: Instead of custom cabinets, change to modular cabinets. Exchange high-end appliances for less expensive products. Change marble to granite or quartz, glass tile to porcelain, farm sink to standard drop-in (cast iron is less money), custom hood to one-piece hood (when shopping for appliances, ask about a package deal). Some manufacturers will give a hood free with the purchase of the range.

Perhaps the plan has too many light fixtures? (Electrical is a big expense since the new requirements of going green and safety.) You can use two 6-inch recess lights for every three 4-inch recesses. Reduce the number of switches (one switch turns on all the bath lights and the ventilation fan, since the fans today are very quiet and helpful for odor and humidity reduction).

Use MDF (modified density fiber) instead of pine or hardwood moldings because after painting, it's not possible to tell the difference. Solid-core room doors are better, but they require three hinges (use hollow core doors with two hinges to save money).

Use picture frame windows (moldings around all four sides) rather than a sill and skirt. Put crown moldings only in primary rooms.

Use fiberglass tubs instead of cast iron. Use framed shower doors or curtains. If you have a one-sided standard shower or a tub/shower, consider a curtain. When slid to one side, it leaves your beautiful shower completely exposed. Shower curtains are coming back!

In place of cabinets with frames, you may have to bite the bullet and use frameless door fronts. Request the contractor leave off the cabinets quote, allowing you to shop around. When it comes to cabinets, the more drawers, the better, but with a higher price tag. Leave off built-in shelving units. You can add this anytime, or perhaps buy a shelving unit at IKEA. Change built-in closet shelving to on-the-job shelving (which costs less).

Make Your Goal List

Stay with the steel chrome closet poles as they are the best. You may want TV cable lines but they soon will be remote. When? You guess when! Perhaps by the time this book gets published.

Change wiring all openings with a security system to motion security.

Sanded hardwood flooring is nice, but soon most flooring will be engineered. (Visit a showroom to see many options.) No new home in a subdivision has anything other than tile or engineered flooring. Be proactive. Better yet, go beyond research.

Carpet is still available but mostly used for second floors. Engineered wood flooring is available layered over cushioned padding, as it makes it quieter.

Okay, so you have a fixed budget but you want the best the industry can offer. You want what you want! When Donald Trump remodeled his Trump Tower Suite, he put in a Kohler K400 toilet. You can purchase this from Home Depot now—or you can have your own throne.

Upgrades (Also See Amenities)

- Island in the kitchen with onyx tile facing and down lighting from under the counter overhang.
- Convection cook top.
- Cabinet glass doors and glass shelves with lighting.
- Custom hood to match fireplace surround using stone.
- Second island or peninsula for food preparation.
- Vegetable sink with disposal and an instant hot faucet.

- Drawer microwave: You can have a second microwave above the oven.

- Separate two-drawer refrigerator under counter (also comes with one drawer).

- Electric opening drawers—just touch to open (no knobs or pulls).

- Built-in small appliance cabinet with fold-up door (appliance garage) for all your coffee needs.

- All drawers, no doors base cabinets (big item to consider).

- Warming drawer, typically installed under oven.

- Country (farm) sink in cast iron or stainless steel.

- Instant hot water at main sink and/or vegetable sink (also known as a food preparation sink).

- Wiring for automobile charger in garage.

- Secondary washing machine in garage for very dirty items.

- Gray water lines from laundry and shower to planted exterior areas.

- Security system.

At this point, you don't exactly know if your plan will be a spa tub/shower or a shower only. The objective is to see what it costs and what order you want to start your budget. Why is this important? More homeowners pay the plan check fee and think this is it. Then along come the building department fees. Surprise to others, but not to you!

Get a total for the plan check fee and all permit fees, including mechanical permit fees (electrical, plumbing, and FAU). While you are at the building department, ask about current code requirements. You don't want to be surprised with lot coverage percentage. Also ask if there are fire sprinkler requirements.

Also important is setback ordinances. Setback is the distance between your house and the property line. There are several that may impact your project. (See below.)

Setbacks

- Setback side yard, if one story.
- Setback side yard, if two story.
- Setback to the street, called *front yard setback*.
- Setback rear to property line.
- Setback to an easement. (Sometimes easements do not come into the rear yard setbacks. You'll want to know.)
- Setback to the road, if private.

Take this list with you and check it off. While there, check to see about electrical meter requirements. You may need an upgrade. If you have a 70-amp meter, you may need an upgrade to at least 200 amp. Ask about any fees for this. Remember, the more answers you get now, the fewer surprises you will have later.

This is Sound Advice

You are slowly becoming knowledgeable. Some departments have separate building and planning departments (also known as a zoning department). While you are there, check with this department. Remember what you find out now will be helpful later on. Most departments are helpful. Ask questions and get answers. It is very possible that when you ask leading questions, this will perk up the clerk to be more receptive.

All you want to do is dance! You want what you want and you want it ASAP. This is fine, but this is the real world. You must put the puzzle together in order to see the complete picture. A big piece of the puzzle is in the budget.

Everyone starts with a budget but most do not detail a buildable budget which requires work and time. It is not as easy as flipping a switch. Would you rather know now or be shocked later?

There will be more to come on kitchen and bath items for the budget. Later, you will show your choices to the architect to design them into the floor plan. Put together a binder. It is not possible to do a complete budget without an itemized binder. This will be your Bible and formulated by you. Be meticulous! Take an active role. You want the best for you.

DEFINITIONS AND DESIGNATIONS

Design with a Vision

Architectural Styles—Victorian, Country French, French Mansard, Contemporary, Modern, Classic, Cape Cod, Tudor, Country Tudor, Mediterranean, Mid-Century Bungalow, Ranch, and Georgian.

Armoire—Tall cupboard wardrobe, free-standing, in bedroom.

Atelier—Gentleman's bedroom (term not used today).

Auto Storage—Garage.

Balcony—Walk out to more easily see below, sitting area, not for entertaining.

Bains Room—Child's room.

Barn Door—Interior sliding door outside the opening.

Bath—A.k.a. bathroom.

Bistro—Smaller 24-inch table, two chairs in master suite or outside near master garden.

Boudoir—Women's private sitting room, dressing room, or bedroom.

Bucolic—Rustic as rustic home site.

Café—Breakfast room.

Cave—Storage.

Coach House—Garage or auto storage (term not used today).

Conservatory—Greenhouse, usually attached to a dwelling for growing and displaying plants.

Console Table—Set against a wall either attached with deco brackets or with legs.

Covered Lanai—Patio room.

Credenza—Sideboard or a cabinet without legs for food tasting.

Cuisine—Kitchen.

Drawing Room—Where visitors may be entertained (not used today).

Dining Room—Salon.

Entry Hall—Interior entry, a.k.a. "foyer," stairs leading up to open area and not a hall.

Energy Room—Yoga center, spa, stretching center, wellness center, workout room.

Eyebrow—Elongated eve roof exterior protruding from building at roof line. Not for structured use. Research.

Finials—Decorative ornament at roof gables.

Foyer—Interior entry; can be at any level.

French Colonial—American version of ornate French, a.k.a. "Country French."

French Mansard—Steep front roof.

Gallery—Artistic work is displayed, a hall.

Garage—A.k.a. "auto storage."

Gathering Room—Family room (term not used on West Coast).

Grand Salon—Drawing room (term not used today).

Inglenook—Bench or corner built-in seat near an open fireplace.

Juliet Balcony—Small balcony without table, standing room only, doors at house, primarily used on second floor.

Junior Suite—Bedroom, same as master but smaller with private bath.

Lair—Pad called living room, resting place (term not used today).

Leisure Room—Family room (term not used today).

Living Room—Grand salon.

Master Café—In a master bedroom, refrigerator, sink and microwave

Master Garden—Smaller walled-in garden primarily visible from master bedroom.

Master Retreat—A room or area, part of the master bedroom.

Master Suite—Large bedroom, master bath with separate tub and shower, walk-in closet and sitting area.

Mid-Century Homes—1930 to 1965.

Mission Style—Spanish or early California style.

Modern Mission—Turn-of-the-century Spanish.

Owners Suite—A.k.a. "master suite."

Parlor—Living room/salon (term not used today).

Pergola—An open shady structure in a yard, sometimes where vines are grown.

Playroom—Sports or recreation room.

Porte-cochère—Carport at side or front of residence on one side attached to house (not allowed close to property line without permission).

Reflecting Pool—Not for swimming or bathing but for fish, turtles, and some plants.

Reflecting Room—Studio/Den.

Stateroom—Formal room for entertaining business guests.

Valet—A stand or rack for holding coats, hats, etc.. Sometimes in a walk-in closet.

Veranda—Covered walkway connection two sections of a building.

Vernacular House—Common architecture of native area house.

Wellness Center—Workout room.

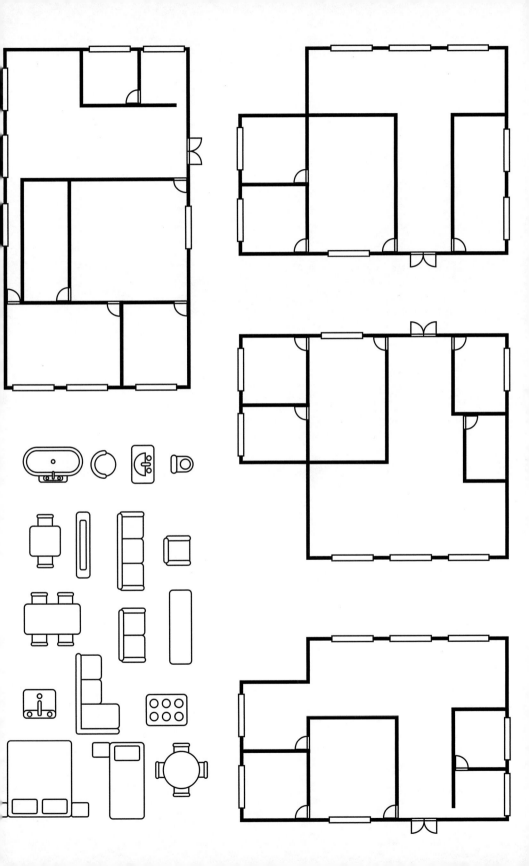

2

Habitable Rooms Plus

Kitchen

Laundry Room

Family / Powder Room

Master Bedroom

Sitting Room

Master Bath

Sauna and Steam Shower

Living Room

Dining Room

Home Office

The Entry

Garage

Hallways and Foyers

Guest Bath & Guest Coat
    Closet

Baths # 2 and 3

Media Center / Recreation
    Room

Wine Cellar

Basement

Solarium vs. Conservatory

Freestanding Structures

Guest House vs. Pool House

Patios and More

Habitable Rooms Plus

KITCHEN

You Live on an Island

Yes, the kitchen is the hub of the house but it was not always. A thousand years ago there was no kitchen—just a fireplace. No running water, no guest seating, only a table and chairs. No cabinets or counters, no tile floors or tile walls, no light fixtures or gas. And of course, no appliances, except the fireplace, which was used for cooking and keeping the house warm.

Cooking was done with wood logs. In larger houses there was a food preparer; in smaller homes, the women of the house did the food preparation.

About the year 200 AD, cabinets from Norway were made, four feet tall and crafted, specifically, to the space available with a wood top. They had doors only, no drawers.

About 650 AD, cabinets were used in kitchens. Cabinets had been made for 1,000 years but they were not in kitchens until the Germans put them in without any particular design. A cabinet was placed randomly and without only open shelving.

Can you believe at the time of our Revolutionary War, we did not have kitchen sinks?

It took another 1,200 years before running water was introduced in the kitchen. That American innovation came about around the year 1875 in New England. That year was significant for the well-being of the general population. In 1875, and after the Revolutionary War, was a good time in our country. The North and South came together quickly and jobs were plentiful for anyone who wanted to work.

In 1880, the kitchen was designated as a room. Previously, it was part of the living room. (What is old is new again!) It was the year innovations took place around the world, but especially in America. By 1895, Americans were ready to begin implementing the new innovations and improved everything from their farm implements to their living conditions.

Electricity Began to Change the Kitchen

During the 1890s, a group formed to oversee the building of homes. They were elected as the *town fathers*. Primarily, they were formed to regulate property boundaries and settle disputes. But when houses burnt down because of faulty ovens, the regulators (later known as the *council*) stepped in and mandated safer ovens.

Ovens were made safer. Okay, what's next?

Anything and everything that can be regulated was regulated. Homeowners objected and objected all the way to the bank. Then came electricity. Can you name the most important innovation and revolution in America?

Okay, you can say the computers, Smartphones, television or the movies. None of these would be possible without the innovation of electricity. Electricity changed the kitchen from workable to convenient.

In 1950, electricity was wonderful, except the icebox needed refilling and heating oil had to be hauled from the basement following the war.

Innovations continued to come at an accelerated pace. Homes were built everywhere.

The Hub of the House is the Kitchen

Everyone wakes and makes their way to the kitchen prior to any other family area. This makes this room special. You should make it look and feel special.

Begin with the location. Aforementioned, the kitchen is to face the rear yard and open to the family room. View to the rear yard and family members in the adjoining room is called an "open kitchen." This is the way today and the future for the middle class.

A lot will change in homes and neighborhoods in a century but the open kitchen will adhere. A century ago, Gerald Jonas said the retractable pen would last a century but with alterations. Case closed.

The upper class has a different arrangement in their new houses: Two kitchens. One is a food preparation kitchen not viewed by guests. This room is to prepare for small or large groups without the noise and odor. The second is an intimate kitchen where friends and relatives can congregate without the ever-present household help.

There is one room used by both the upper and middle class. It's the butler's pantry. Not at all a pantry, it is a walk through room between the kitchen and dining room. Upper class has all the amenities, which include cabinets with glass doors, plenty of drawers, full height cabinets for storage, under-counter refrigerator and wine cooler cabinet, sink (main sink and vegetable sink, also known as a preparation sink), and plenty of counter space with a large window.

The middle class butler's pantry has glass door cabinets, a counter with no windows, and sometimes a sink. You want more. Don't do it. This room must be proportionate to the rest of the house. An island in the kitchen is a must. No question about it. Period. The placement of the island is so crucial for modern livability and resale. The island can seat a minimum of two and a maximum of four. Not more than four. Period! (Lots of periods in this section.) You live on an island.

No matter how large your island is, there should be seating for only four. Every seat takes 24" of space so an island of four is to be a minimum of 8 feet. You can put appliances on this island top, but only two—the cooktop and the vegetable sink. No other. Not the main sink. Period. Do not put the sink on the island. The reason for this is that the seating at the island is to face the rear yard windows and be adjacent to the family room. This way, anyone seated can see the view outside and also anyone in the family room without turning completely around. The concept is the only way to go but is seldom done. About 90% of islands have their backs to the family room. The designers say this is more intimate. It keeps the kitchen separate.

You invested so much to get an open kitchen, why consider intimacy? What you really want is togetherness. Why have your back to your friends? The author hopes this 90% will diminish with time. Who knows?

Do not put the sink on an island facing the seating. Visualize the dirty dishes. Enough said. The main kitchen sink should face the rear yard. Period! You must be able to watch the little ones while you are at the sink. Even while cooking, you will return from time to time to the sink. Sinks come in white cast iron and stainless steel. Stainless has been the current choice. You can choose either an under mount or a farm style. Soon available will be various colored stainless steel sinks—black is available now.

An *instant hot* is a big investment but you will love it as it will give you instant tea or coffee as well as soup. Take advantage of living in The Golden Age. It won't be long before these designs will become universal.

Cooking appliances are divided into various components. There is the freestanding range, the built-in oven (along with microwave and warming drawers), the drop-in cook top, slide-in range, drawer microwave, refrigerator and freezer, drawer refrigerator, and hoods or ventilating hoods.

The author does not suggest one appliance layout over another, but you should do your due diligence. The smaller the kitchen, the smaller the appliances. Large kitchen? Plan for larger or more units.

Hoods are to be at least 6" wider than the cook top. A 36" cook top should have a 42" wide hood. Looks good. Hoods are not required by many departments but it is a good idea to put a ventilating fan in the ceiling nearby. Manufacturers suggest hoods to be 30" above the cooktop, but the author suggests 36" is better. You don't want to hit your head.

Share the Love

Number one on your wish list are the cabinets. This is where nearly all homeowners go wrong. Many homeowners order modulated, off-the-shelf cabinets. You will never get a final good kitchen because they, no matter what is told to you, do not have everything you need. Some do come close. This author has never seen cabinets purchased and installed by a home center to be more than 75% proper.

What are proper cabinets? There are three types of cabinets: base, wall, and tall. These cabinets have either drawers or door fronts. The sink cabinet should have two doors, and the vegetable sink, if you have one. All other base cabinets should have drawers only: a smaller drawer at the top and a larger one below, or a tier of four equal drawers. No pull out shelves. Period!

The trash compartment should pull out and not have a drawer. Any corner cabinet should have a lazy Susan. Research the various types and styles. Consider glass door cabinets along the end of a large island, but be sure they are tempered.

Wall cabinets are best 42" maximum height for an 8' ceiling and 54" for a 9' ceiling. If you have a 9' ceiling, you can have the upper 12" with glass-front doors that are lighted for displaying turners. Also, a couple of glass doors for display with lights elsewhere, but not close to the sink. Period! Wall cabinets next to the sink are for everyday use and not for show. Don't let the beauty of lighted glass-front cabinets get in the way of practicability. Be honest with yourself. You can put these above the refrigerator, or any other place except next to the sink. All shelves to be melamine to avoid sticking.

Countertops are to be stone. Period! You can also put in part butcher block counters. Stone is the choice of 95% of homeowners, and therefore, the best for resale. The backsplash (wall area between the counter and wall cabinets) is to be tiled with subway tile or other decorative tile.

When You Tear Out Your Kitchen, There is No Turning Back

Sinks to be under mount for easy cleaning. Top mount sinks went out with the dinosaurs. The instant hot is a must. Soap dispensers are an option. Faucets to match your décor, but a spray attachment at the sink is advisable.

Hanging lights above the island, a must. (Also, above the sink as an option.) Use recess LED lights only in task areas, not in walking areas. Period! No dimmers in kitchen. Period. Switches on the island for these lights is convenient. Also, put an outlet on both sides of a larger island (more than 5'). A television monitor connected to your family room TV is fun. Put in a mute mode on the island.

As for flooring in the kitchen, anything goes as long as it is water resistant. Polyurethane on natural wood works but it is only 75% water resistant. If water spills on the floor, you need to clean it up anyway.

Windows in the kitchen should be 4' by 4' to the side yard and larger to the backyard but the wider the window, the less space you have for wall cabinets and the farther to put away items from the sink—trade-off!

A walk-in pantry is desired by everyone. Try to put one in. If they design it well, it will fit in about 30% of homes. The resale value is not significant. An option is roll out, full height cabinets for pantry items. Research.

This author knows there are unending items to be addressed for kitchens. Manufacturers have R&D departments costing millions to come up with the best value for you. But this author guarantees the aforementioned will enhance your lifestyle and your pocketbook.

Bamboo cabinets, least known today, will be the cabinets of choice for kitchens and baths. Bamboo is the utmost quality wood you can use. Today, bamboo is costly but soon the price will come down the way of flat screen TVs. Natural or stained darker, this fabulous wood will come through for entire kitchens in bamboo or partial, such as the island only.

Research bamboo. You can have the future kitchen look today. Shaker in bamboo, no problem. Bamboo is sustainable. It is not a tree, it is a grass that grows fifteen feet in just three years. Bamboo is grown on farms. When cut to ground level, it will sprout 15 feet. Unlike other hardwoods that take 100 years to mature, bamboo recycles itself and does not require replanting. Good for appearance as well as the environment. Go Green! Go bamboo! Research *Décor-Active*.

This is Good Advice

For thousands of years, families were deprived of a breakfast room, all the way up to the end of the 20th century. Homes had a dining table for all meals. Then along came the American businessman and the morning newspaper. The children sat at a table to do homework, but not at the dining table. The breakfast room was born!

Modern architects, challenged to accommodate their clients' requests, had to find a place to put this additional room or area. Unfortunately, they missed the boat. They wrongfully put the breakfast room (table) between the kitchen and family room. Wrong!

Developers are paying designers big bucks for something so wrong. Never should one walk through a room or designated area to get to another room. Walk through the breakfast room to get to the family room. Missing the boat. This table sometimes has a direct view to the rear yards. The breakfast room can only be used for breakfast? Da!

When two guests arrive, they would appreciate a small setting with you. The breakfast table works well.

The breakfast room should be set alongside the kitchen and family room to create a triangle. Kitchen + Family Room + Breakfast Room. Never incorporate the breakfast room into the kitchen. Always have it facing the rear yard. There is nothing better than to read the paper early in the morning or to review your itinerary of the day with the view of your wonderful backyard before going to work.

Check Emails Over Coffee

Then the children come and sit near you for breakfast. They will not appreciate the backyard but will like the table to be separated. Oh yes! There is the island. This author suggests opening the island for use after 8:30 a.m. Use the breakfast room until then. You rebuilt your house with a strategic plan; now it's time to plan your lifestyle.

This may mean, when you plan your layout, that you will need to extend the breakfast room to accommodate the family into the rear of the house. You can decorate this room with a small chandelier. It will increase your property value. Awake to the power of good design.

This author comments on eating: You can eat in the dining room or the breakfast room, but with the hurry-up lifestyle of today, eating is at the island and in the family room while watching TV at the coffee table. McDonalds is knocking. Watching TV at the breakfast table can be done with a small wall TV or a small monitor showing the same as the family room TV.

LAUNDRY ROOM

Laundry Chutes and Clotheslines

It wasn't too long ago that the laundry room was a part of the kitchen or a back opening porch, using a scrub board and two rollers to squeeze out water. Clothes were hung on a clothesline with close pins. Clothes pins were invented by the Shakers in the early 1800s. They consisted of a cylindrical piece of wood with a vertical notch cut into the bottom.

In 1853, an American put together a two-piece spring-loaded lever clothes pin made of beech wood. These pins still are in use today and have many operations. But its reputation is still on the line.

This author, as a kid, improvised rubber shooting guns made with clothes pins—discarded rubber inner tubes cut like rubber bands stretched on a 2" by 6" block of wood and hooked into a clothes pin. Pushing down on the wooden pin would release the rubber band and it would fly as far as 20 feet. Not at all harmful and lots of fun for kids. This toy went out with the cap gun in 1950, but clothes pins are still available for hanging clothes. Would you believe it?

Today, no more toy guns. What is the world coming to? Probably a good thing!

In the 1940s, when one's wife received the first actual washing machine, she jumped with joy. No more hard scrubbing, just load the clothes in the washing tub, add soap and flip the switch. All there was to do was hang the washing on a clothes line with clothes pins. All backyards had clothes lines. The modern ones in the 40s had a line that reeled in the clothes as they were removed by putting a pulley at either end. The shower curtain rod also doubled for drying.

Then along came the electric dryer, invented in 1915. The housewife jumped with joy when the appliance arrived with the advent of the washer. She did a double-flip when the dryer arrived. No more clothes pins, no more hanging out the clothes in the cold.

Clean Clothes Come from Here

But the downside was lack of electricity coming from the 30-amp panel. The entire house used 30 amps! No electrical room for a dryer.

This was a boom for electricians all over the country, changing out the panel to 70 amps to accommodate. At the average wage, it took 500 hours of work to pay for it. Those living in apartments (flats, as they were called then) relied on the building owner to foot the cost and that came with an increase of rent. It was a modern investment.

This travesty was quickly solved with the gas dryer. From post-war to 1970, gas and electric hookups were installed because when a family moved in, they would bring their gas and electric dryers with them.

Then, in the mid 70s, gas was mostly used because the energy cost was lower, and there was already gas to the house to supply the house heating system.

Where gas was not available, electric dryers had to be used. But gas is prevalent in this country. There is enough gas underground to service this country for the next 1,000 years.

Back to the electric dilemma of not enough power from the panel. Prior to the breakers, as we know them now, there were screw-in fuses. The dryer could not take the electrical surge needed to energize it. That meant direct line circuit breakers.

Homeowners had to choose between drying their clothes or chancing a fire. Most chose upping their insurance. Then along came the 100 amperage exterior electrical box with flip circuits instead of the screw in, and everyone began to breathe again, especially the firefighters.

What is Right for You?

In the early 1960s, laundromats popped up all over the country, primarily serving apartment renters and those yet to have proper electrical to meet their needs. Today, laundromats are fading since all homes, condos, and apartments are required to have safe equipment.

Then along came the laundry room. Every house built since 1917 made provisions for a laundry room. This room was as small as possible and off the kitchen. The majority of laundry rooms had an exterior door to the backyard and also a window, and occasionally a laundry tub (also called a laundry tray). Everyone loved this arrangement.

When home shoppers saw these arrangements, they would inevitably say, "This is the house for me." After all, what could be better than a laundry next to the kitchen where both cooking and laundry could be done simultaneously? The electric dryer was invented in 1915 and was 6000 watts.

Then along came the misinformed homeowner. Why not make the kitchen larger by extending it into the laundry room and put the washer and dryer in the garage or patio? Why not? The neighbors did it.

In all fairness to homes built prior to 1955, there was no space in the house to put the laundry appliance except in the garage, and in some cases, the patio.

This widespread idea lasted until they went to sell their house. The discriminating home buyer said, "Why should I buy this house and go out in the rain to fetch clothes from the laundry machine? No way Jose." If only the stackable washer and dryer had been invented. There may have been room somewhere to put them inside at the time.

Now we have come from a wash tub to a modern laundry room. An ideal laundry room has a place for a washer and dryer, side by side. A stacked unit is good for limited space, such as condos and guest houses. There are also provisions for a hamper or two to separate clothes, a counter for folding, and/or a counter of stone or wood over the two units (this should be about 60" x 36"), but it's to be about 38" from the floor, 2" above normal counter height (for folding use, the height may not be a factor), and with a laundry tray, either freestanding or built-in. If you build in the laundry tray (sink), there is space under for cabinet storage, wall cabinets for storage and/or open shelves. A bar for hand drying needs to be 24", minimum.

If you can afford the space, extend the counter to a sitting area for crafts use. And don't forget the window. You need to see what's happening while folding clothes. The laundry has come a long way.

Then along came the laundry chute. The laundry chute dates back to King Henry VIII, who threw his laundry from his window to the servants below to launder. His queen laid down the law: Don't throw your clothes out the window anymore. Period.

The King later beheaded the queen. But he had remorse and requested his engineers to put in a laundry chute to the bottom floor. Voila! This worked out great! At a subsequent ball, he suggested this to other aristocrats and many took up the renovation.

Then along came the developer. After investing a great deal of money determining what the modern homeowner wants, they, among other planners, came up with the laundry room to end all laundry rooms. Until something better!

Today, if you have a two-story house, you will want a laundry chute. A laundry chute is probably the most convenient part of your house and a welcomed entity. The chute consists of a door to a cabinet without a bottom (that's the chute). You open the door and put clothes in the chute and you're done. The dirty clothes drop below into either a wall cabinet or a tall cabinet that goes to a basket or hamper where the clothes can be sorted and laundered.

Bottom line: If you want ultra-convenience, a laundry chute could be a big selling point in the future. Be sure to make the initial opening less than 100 square inches so children do not try to use it as a slide chute. They will get caught part way down. Additionally, put a safety latch on the door.

FAMILY / POWDER ROOM

Modern Living

The family room is relatively new to residential homes. The family room trumped the living room circa 1960. The living room gave way to the family room since it's open to the kitchen. This takes us full circle to a century ago when the stove and living room with a table was part of every room. The table was for dining, any time of day.

So now the family room and kitchen are one. It's called an "open kitchen." Some thought about the turn of the 20th century, that a wall between the kitchen and family room was a good idea, since it keeps cooking odors out of the family room. Not true. Odors will travel through the doorway and make this argument moot.

Also, during this same time period, designers thought a wall would keep guests out of the kitchen. When this did not happen, the wall came tumbling down, resulting, visually, in a large room made up of a kitchen and family room combination.

Consider how often guests are in this area, compared to your family. Now, one can watch what is going on everywhere while standing at the sink. This is called "modern living."

The position of the island comes into play here but will be addressed with the kitchen. If you have only one TV in the house, this is where it belongs. If you have multiple TVs, this TV should be visible from all parts of the kitchen.

A fireplace is also in order. Place the TV above the fireplace. A family room without a TV above the fireplace is not fully dressed. If a guest walks into this room, they will get the feeling that something is wrong. They won't know what but their instincts will tell them that the room is not complete. No fireplace or TV? These people missed the boat.

Again, revisit the idea of a resale.

A Place for Comfort

On the floor plan, position the fireplace/TV in direct view of the kitchen on the farthest wall. The space between the kitchen and fireplace is for furniture. No eating at the table but viewing seating. (This means the breakfast table should not be situated between the kitchen and family rooms.) This is very hard for experienced designers to come to grips with. But they will when the majority prevails in the near future.

Putting a breakfast table between the kitchen and family room is like covering half of your front car window. You may still see out, but how annoying!

This table goes elsewhere (see breakfast room section).

Draw a line on your plan. Connect the kitchen sink to the fireplace/TV. Are there any obstructions? There cannot be. Don't just let a quick design get in the way of the facts. What size fireplace? What size TV? The answer is as large as possible. But remember, this is not a media center or a fireplace to heat the house, so be proportionate.

Next, draw on your plan furniture: couch or couches, chair or chairs or sectional. The optimal distance for a coffee table (formerly called a cocktail table) should have at least a 15" clearance between it and any seating. This may seem close but it's utilitarian when setting down drinks or food. Yes food. Times have changed and many of the younger generation prefer to watch TV while having a meal or snacking. This author pleads guilty.

Think about the younger generation at all times for they will shape the house design of the future.

Lighting should consist of mostly canister ceiling lights. Do not put hanging light fixtures that will impede vision from the kitchen. Lights have three objectives: First is to light the whole room. Place your lights 3' 6" from the wall and install them with dimmers. Next is the ambiance lighting. Perhaps pendants on both sides of the TV with smaller bulbs (15 amps). Also convenience lights between the kitchen and family room.

In the event that you have unlimited funds and have a high ceiling, you can put a dome in the center with a light fixture that lowers with a switch made by Aladdin Company. This author did it and it lowers with a remote to clean it. A wow with guests!

You want surround sound? Then you came to the right place. A low voltage company can suggest where to play it. Also, perhaps you want to watch TV from the kitchen, but the volume to hear is too high?

Answer: Put a volume control on the island with a ceiling speaker. You are now living life to the fullest!

MASTER BEDROOM
Live Life Better!

The feature furniture in the master bedroom is the bed. (Now you know how astute the author is!)

The bed should be as large as possible and accommodate two night stands. Night stands can be matching but don't need to be. Additional space should be left at the foot of the bed or bed bench to a dresser, fireplace or wall up to a maximum of three feet, six inches. The foot of the bed should face a wall at least the width of the bed. For instance, if the bed is five feet wide, the wall should be at least five feet wide.

The wall can be used for a cabinet with a flat screen TV or a fireplace with a TV above. If you don't want a TV in the bedroom now, you should still allocate space for it in the future, God forbid someone is bedridden and cannot be easily moved. Having a TV in the bedroom is a good way to pass the time. If nothing else, having a monitor to see who is at the front door or anywhere else in the house will be helpful. The biggest reason to make this provision now is resale. When the house goes up for sale, the agent can turn on the TV and show an aquarium of fish or landscape scenes—crowd pleaser! And those walking through your house will remember the possibilities.

Another alternative is to make provisions for a TV, but for now, use the wall space for a painting. If possible, you can get a local artist to paint a 48" by 36" painting of the front or rear of your house after it is completed. I would offer them $350.00 to do this. Should you, instead, want to go with an inexpensive option, Ravensburger makes fantastic 3,000-piece puzzles that can be mounted and framed. Check out puzzle No. 17069-2, which measures 48" x 32" plus the frame at 4". (I know because I have one in progress.) Ravenburger estimates that it will take 140 hours to put together. Be sure to finish it off with a frame with glass to hold the pieces in place.

Is there anywhere else you can place the foot of the bed? Nowhere else! Never should it face the door of the bedroom or any other door, especially not the bath door. It should not face the backyard windows. If you look at any hotel today, you will see this is a uniform practice. The hotels' placement of beds should end this conversation.

Draw a furniture plan and place the bed. If the bed does not fit properly, work on it until it does. Regardless of what your Feng Shui practitioner tells you, these are proper design tips. The space left over, after the main ingredient, can accommodate a dresser, book shelf cabinet, chaise lounge, a potted plant, or a small table with two chairs.

The bed, since it's facing the wall, will be adjacent to the backyard window or doors. Here, put as much glass as possible, but no balcony. A balcony will obstruct your vision of the yard below. The one exception is a Juliet balcony if you are on the second floor. Make sure it has depth of no more than two feet from the exterior wall. That is enough space to walk out, smoke, take in the fresh air, and look down to see the dog digging up your roses.

There are only three doors in the master bedroom (four, if you have a sitting room). They are the entry door, the door to the bath, and the door to the walk-in closet. Wardrobes are out—I mean out. You must have a walk-in closet; it does not have to be large.

The walk-in closet advantage is in seeing everything when standing inside. The closet is to have three elements—four, if you have the space. Shelf and poles for both double-hanging short items, such as shirts, and shelving for shoes, folded sweaters, bags, and hats. Also, it should have a tier of drawers and single-hanging poles for long items.

The floor below the shelving can also be used for shoes. If you have the space, built-in cabinets are in order here. If you put in these cabinets, make the top drawer or two only four inches deep and line with felt for jewelry. If you have expensive jewelry, then request cabinets to be made with an open proof drawer that only you know how to open. This jewelry drawer can also be incorporated in a bedroom cabinet. You may have insurance, but you can never replace a pendant given to you by your grandmother. Another option is to install a built-in safe.

Lighting and Its Effects

Proper lighting is both utilitarian and aesthetic. The closet should have a motion light. A switch is good, but a motion light is quicker. Bedroom lighting comes in three types:

A center light, used for housekeeping, will light the entire room. Also a fan/light combination can be used.

Next are the LED canister lights, which are placed 3' 6" from each wall (remember the 3' 6" dimension?). This dimension is used throughout the interior of the house. The 3' 6" is to be set no matter what size the bedroom is. Lights above the bed should also be canister style but limited to 4 inches.

If you choose to not have lights above the bed, then each nightstand needs a lamp. A light above the TV is not in order, as it was a decade ago. But if you do not have a TV, and instead have a wall picture, then an eyeball light will be good with a separate switch.

The switches are placed for your convenience. The lights above the bed should be controlled from either side of the bed. A switch at the room entrance should also turn on all lights. It's called a three-way, even though only two switches are involved. The center lights switch on only from the entry.

If you have a walk-up bar then use a separate switch and light. Any other additional areas also should have a separate switch. You should be able to switch on the lights as you enter a room and switch them off from the bed. This makes life simple.

Consider sound-deadening walls between the bedroom and the bath. This can be achieved by using sound-deadening insulation and sound-deadening drywall. It is costly but if you can work it into your budget, you may sleep easier. It's not soundproof but deadens sound. You may still hear screams, but not normal talking. Soon, there will be a silent toilet when flushing.

If you have extra space in the bedroom area and your budget is bigger than average, you may want to create a sitting area or one just off the bedroom. The sitting room is for sitting: enjoying a good book (preferably mine!), or for watching TV. This is sometimes called a "man cave," where you can watch a football game or the news of the day.

SITTING ROOM

Solitude

The sitting room can be private or semi-private, situated off the master bedroom only. This room has also changed over the years from a room to a study and from reading a book to also include a fireplace and TV. You can add a bookshelf here, as large as can fit.

Smaller windows are okay since view is not the function of this room. Your bedroom faces the rear, therefore, windows may not be possible. Not a problem!

The ideal sitting room has double-pocket doors, which can remain open, enlarging the bedroom. These doors can be solid or glass. Only your architect will know.

The sitting room requires minimum light. There is no need for dimmers; only task lighting for reading or watching TV is needed.

A wet bar is in order with a very small sink, small refrigerator, and cabinets.

Most homes cannot accommodate the luxury of a sitting room but a sitting room in the master bedroom may be possible.

The sitting room is generally used by one person, therefore, it needs little furnishing: a sofa or lounge chair and a TV. Put in a fireplace—why not? Two fireplaces in the master suite? Do it upscale!

The bottom line here is to create comfortable living. We all realize that we have limited time on this planet, so let's live life to its fullest.

MASTER BATH

When Planning, Go Beyond to do the Right Thing

You have planned a perfect kitchen for your house. Now you want an equally well-placed master bath. If a guest visits your house and walks into a beautiful kitchen, they will wonder, "How nice is the master bath?" That's because a great kitchen goes hand-in-hand with a great master bath.

In this country, the name of this room is bath. In other countries, this room is called bathroom or toilet. Commercially, this country calls it a restroom. "Bathroom" is still used in homes today, but for design purposes, the name is simply "bath."

After the kitchen and the master bedroom, the master bath needs the most thought. Size is not a factor. What is important is what's in and around the room.

Position the room with the main window facing the rear yard, one entry door and perhaps a door to the closet or closets. If there is a door to a closet, then there is to be another door from the closet to the bedroom.

Hidden from sight is the toilet and/or bidet. They should be out of sight from the doorway when entering the bath. If space allows, add a dividing wall or a toilet compartment. Soon you will see, in larger homes, another washbasin in this compartment room.

Have one or two washbasins as space permits. Don't crowd two basins in a space of less than a six foot cabinet. Counter space is more valuable than two washbasins.

For years, this unit has been called a "vanity unit." The makeup vanity is a place to sit only for a short time. Sometimes, the makeup vanity is called a vanity. Confusing? But isn't this all?

There must be a separate tub and shower. You are putting together a master suite. A suite consists of the largest bedroom in the house, a walk-in closet—not a wardrobe—and a master bath, which is serviced from the bedroom only, and not any other outside room except a sitting room. It is the largest bathroom in the house, with a separate tub and shower. Anything less is not considered a master suite.

If space is limited, make the tub as small as 12.5 square feet (30" x 60") and the shower nine square feet (36" x 36"). Increase these sizes depending on how much room you have, realizing that the shower is used many times more than the tub.

Installing a tub with a spa connection is a luxury you may not want to overlook. Besides the refreshing feeling, you get the cost back many times over in resale value.

Soaking and Freestanding Tubs

Every potential buyer looks into the tub to see if it has spa provisions. (See section on steam shower and sauna.)

Freestanding tubs are returning. Some have spa connections but most do not. These are called "soaking tubs." This tub comes with or without faucet provisions. The original soaking tubs were introduced about 1865. These units had only the valves (faucets) outside the tub. They are now available with the valves built in to the deck, which does not show the pipes coming up from the floor. Either is acceptable to the discriminating buyer.

Having the valves exposed is more 20th century and traditional. Concealed valves is a more modern look. Also available for all type tubs are spouts coming from the ceiling. Research this. A freestanding tub will take up more space. Most designers don't allow enough space around the tub. The rule is that if your tub is six feet wide, then it must have a seven foot space.

Tile the floor under the tub and the walls 12" minimum above the tub on all sides. This is called wainscot tiling. Most master tubs are built-in and tiled 12" higher around three sides.

You have the space to put in a step. The downside is that getting into the tub is more of a crawling effort than stepping. Where does a bat go to clean? The bath tub.

John Glenn, senator and astronaut, stepped into his tub and broke his leg. Save a leg by installing a grab bar. Also, most faucet spouts are strong enough to hold on to.

How much space do you need for the tub? The largest tub is 48" x 72" or 24 square feet. Anything larger and you will sink. This is a two-person tub or a place for the kids to sail boats or play with crocodiles.

Little boy asked his mom, "Why do I need a bath? Can I just be vacuumed?"

Stone should be used flat around a built-in tub. A one-piece stone will always work. Back and sides can be tiled or stone can be used, but it is not necessary. If you use tile or stone, then no more than 12" is necessary above the tub. If you have a window, then put the window close to the tub for aesthetics. Window treatments should be either waterproof or should not cover the window. If you are on the second floor, then you have the luxury of privacy.

Since you are going upscale, then why not put in a TV and electric fireplace? Both should be visible and controlled from the tub. While you're at it, put in surround sound. This tub may be seldom used but the attention to detail will be appreciated. The tub is visually the focal point of the room. Sometimes, this feature will sell the house or at least get you your asking price. Resale is every-thing! So many homes are built or remodeled with less than these features and they become ordinary. Do you want to be ordinary?

Can You Fathom That?

Is this author fanatical about details and good design? Absolutely. Remember, no switches or outlets are to be reachable from inside the tub. Safety first!

Only 150 years ago we did not have indoor showers. Can you fathom that? What would life be like without a shower? Nearly 85% of all homes outside of this country do not have a shower. Many upscale hotels around the world have upgraded to a tub with a hand-held shower. Well, again, what makes us the leaders in the free world? Innovation. As much as the companies try, they cannot convince the rest of the world that a shower is the better way of life.

Benjamin Franklin, statesman, inventor, and one of our founding fathers, never took a shower. He bathed every day, hand washing himself. With all of his inventive abilities, he did not come close to inventing the shower.

The shower was invented by Hans Marsintie of the Nether-lands, but it did not become popular around the world at that time. There were activists then, as there are now, and they believed that the shower would use too much water, and with the added burden of it having to be heated, it was considered unheard of waste.

The shower did not become common until heating oil was processed. This inception made living conditions change drastically. However, after the war, many apartments still had no provisions for hot water. Oil was used primarily for heating and cooking.

Until about 1958, families heated a tea kettle on the stove and then poured hot water into the tub. Can you imagine how long that took?

Then along came gas, and with it, the water heater that produced hot water for showers. At first, the activists screamed that showers used too much expensive water and gas. Not at all true. A shower, on average, takes eight minutes—eight minutes of running hot water. A bath, on the other hand, requires four times as much water and gas. Here we are, less than 100 years later, and every home has a shower and a gas water heater.

The tankless heater was invented by Takaki of Japan. Many also claimed this invention. Like many inventions, it was an evolution waiting to be discovered.

The Face of Beauty

Let's proceed from the basics to the ultimate or near ultimate. Most all manufacturers make upgraded shower assemblies. The first added feature to the shower is the handheld shower head. This requires a diverter to move from an overhead shower spray to a handheld, generally on a rod that can be raised and lowered to a desirable height. This can be used as a body spray, regular shower head, or used to clean the shower, since it has a flexible cable line of six feet.

Want to go very upscale? Then install a digital shower made by Kohler®. No handles, no knobs, just push buttons. Set the temperature you want. It can be controlled from both inside and outside the shower.

While you are at it, put in a foot massager. You have the money, why not?

Also, a rain shower above with a diverter. Keep in mind that all cannot be used at once due to most regulations. Punch in what you want and change as you wish. And again, research.

Even if you have a small shower, put in a low corner shelf to be used by Lady Schick. But don't put in a seat in a small shower. There is not enough standing space. Showers of the future will have glass panels surrounding them but no shower door. It's happening now.

Let's say you are removing a tub and want to put in a shower only. Tubs are 5 feet wide. This is large for general use. Now you can install a seat at one end. This will reduce the shower to about 3 feet. Three feet is enough space for a shower. The seat at the opposite end of the shower valve acts as a spot for relaxation or if you can plumb it properly, a foot massage, the installation of which is left to you and your contractor. This seat can be warmed by electric wiring, controlled outside the shower.

With the ultimate shower, what's next? Shower doors. Frameless shower doors work with any style house. Today, shower doors are available with self-cleaning glass. Your housekeeper should charge you less!

Ventilating fans are a must in every bath but if you have a large master bath, install or incorporate two vent fans. Panasonic makes fans so quiet you don't know they are on. When you enter the bath, turn on one switch to light the bath and activate the fans. This will keep your bathroom free from mildew and odor. It will also reduce steam on mirrors.

Tank water heaters are as outdated as the Ford Model T. The tankless water heater is a huge savings for the homeowner because it uses far less gas to heat the pipes. Both types take just as long for water to get to your fixtures but the tank heater heats up even when not in use. In cold climates, this could be cost prohibitive for the average homeowner. The tankless water heater heats only when you turn on the faucet. This is a major factor when you are away from home. Again, the tank heater works when you are not there while the tankless works only when you use it.

For large homes (more than two bathrooms) consider more than one tankless. The hot water will get to the areas with a shorter line. The more tankless units you install, the higher the savings will be. There is no better investment for your home project. Also be aware some heaters will service three or more baths and a laundry without running cold. Research. Showers today are more and more innovative. From the valves to turn on the shower and a shower head, to body sprays and foot massagers.

Vanities and Lighting

You don't need excessive lighting in a bath; what you need is task lighting. Light the vanity area properly. A recess light in the ceiling is good but not effective. Put wall sconces on both sides of the sink where the man who shaves and the woman putting on makeup can use it effectively.

Put a ceiling light above the toilet; the reader will love it. Put a light fixture, not a recess light, in the center of the room. You'll love it.

Put a light in or outside the shower. Someone will love it.

Install an exhaust fan near the shower to prevent steaming up mirrors. There is nothing more annoying than to exit the shower and see the mirrors are steamed.

A vanity is better served with a sconce on both sides and a pendant light above. Modern hotels have good vanity lighting. Take a page from this: A hanging light above the tub adds romance and can be put on a dimmer.

With all these lights you will need switches. The fewer switches, the better. This means one switch should light up multiple areas. You be the judge. The argument for fewer switches is remembering which is which. Using LED keeps the cost low. (See LED in the Energy chapter.)

Design cabinets with a minimum of 12" of counter space on either side of the sink. This means a one basin cabinet should be a total width of 3' 6" minimum. A two basin cabinet should be 72" minimum. Less is crowded. The 3' 6" unit should have four drawers.

Separate his and hers units are most acceptable. One drawer is to have an outlet in the wall at the back of one top drawer to allow a hair dryer so not to plug in each time.

Affordable Luxury

Tile and stone are a part of every master bath with stone counters and stone around the built-in tub. Stone slabs on shower walls are expensive and not attractive (unless you live in Vermont, next to a quarry).

Stone is good for a counter. A backsplash should be no more than 5" above the counter. Stone walls around a shower are now available in 3/8" thickness, which is the same as most tile. If you do not want grout, then this is for you. But keep in mind in this day and age, most home buyers are looking at subway tile, also called staggered set tile, is a style of tile seen in all the subways in major metropolitan cities built in the early 20th century.

Tile walls around the tub 12" and on shower walls, preferably, white subway staggered from 2" x 4" to 4" x 12". The larger the tile, the easier it is to clean. Some tile is available with no cleaning grouts. Research.

Nevertheless, tile for shower floors is to be 1" x 1" mosaic or 2" by 2" (both come in sheets). The purpose for this smaller tile is non-slip. Here is where grout is helpful to prevent slipping. Stone does not work. Period!

The floor of the bath can use a minimum of 12" x 12" tile. Larger tile is acceptable also stone tile works well with a big budget.

Hardwood floors, engineered type water-resistant materials, fit into the current scope of things. The composite flooring is not waterproof but water-resistant. If you want wood, why not use tile that looks like wood. This is the tile of the future. Don't miss out. Research.

Shower Doors, Fans, and More

Don't use frosted, opaque, or obscure glass on windows. There are many manufacturers making remote-control curtains, or simply use curtains with rods or shades.

The same holds true for shower doors. There should be no obstruction to view the tile work through clear frameless glass. It is more costly than framed shower doors and it now comes with self-cleaning glass. Thicker glass of at least 3/8" with ½" works better. Look at it this way, every hotel room built today has clear frameless glass shower doors, no matter what the style of the units or the resort.

A shampoo shelf, at least 12" x 12" is best placed under the shower head so showering water spray will not be affected.

Queen Victoria said she takes a bath once a month—whether she needs it or not.

Ventilating fans come 25, 50, or 110 CFM. This means the air changes every five minutes with 25 CFM (cubic feet per minute). In larger baths, two ventilating fans are in order. If the number and size fans are used, then the mirrors will not fog. But also available are non-fogging mirrors. Research.

Remember to make provisions for access to tub motors controlling the spa.

The final item is a full-height mirror. Remember, no mirrors in the bedrooms, but in the bath it is a necessity. Put the mirror on the wall or one or two sides of a door. The door to the toilet compartment is a good location. You can use a freestanding mirror, if you have the room and it's not obstructing.

Today, towel bars are used less. Folded towels on a wall rack are becoming more popular. The rack can be put anywhere, especially above the toilet. On the whole, treat you bath as if it were a business, a business for profit—maybe even install two toilets in the master bath.

SAUNA AND STEAM SHOWER

Steam Rises

Have you ever wondered about the health benefits of using a sauna or a steam room? Many of us enjoy these treatments at our local health club or spa because they feel good after a tough workout or a long day at the office. But it turns out that using these heated rooms can provide certain health and medical advantages, as well.

Caution: If you have heart disease, check with your doctor before going into a steam shower, sauna, spa tub, or an outside Jacuzzi, and check the time to be safe.

A sauna can be as small as a two-person room. Place the sauna inside the bath or outside the bath, accessible from a hall. Inside the master bath is best. Also, the pool house is good, either inside the building or outside with a separate door.

A traditional sauna provides dry heat. Depending on the sauna you use, you might experience moisture as low as 10% or as high as 60%. The amount of moisture you experience is dependent on the sauna style you choose. Some saunas allow you to increase the humidity by pouring water on lava rocks to create steam.

The traditional saunas consists of four elements:

1. A glass door.
2. Sauna electric heater with lava rocks to create steam, temperature control, and a display to adjust the heat when desired.
3. Seat for at least two, covered with walls, floor, and a ceiling with unfinished cedar wood.
4. A light with a dimmer controlled outside the sauna.

A steam shower is also called a Turkish-style bath. Steam rooms are designed to accommodate 95%-100% humidity. The temperature in a steam room may range from 100-120 degrees Fahrenheit, but it may feel warmer because of the high humidity.

In some steam rooms, you'll find a spray bottle of eucalyptus oil or another scent to enhance your steam experience. Because steam rises, you'll find that sitting higher in a steam room provides more intense heat and steam while sitting lower in the steam room offers less steam and heat.

A Place for Tranquility

A steam shower is of two varieties: First, building a glass shower enclosure to the ceiling will give you a good enclosed steam room. An opening as large as can be constructed should be operable from inside the shower to let off steam for regular shower use. Best to put a ventilating fan in the ceiling outside the shower stall.

The steam room is also known as a "sweat room." For a more intense steam, put in a steam unit controlled in the shower with a timer. This unit can be located in the attic, closet, or outside the shower.

Inside the steam shower, a seat is a must, and can be heated with an exterior switch near the light. Caution: Mark the switch so that it will not be left on. Better to put it on a timer so as not to burn out the electrical elements.

Anyone who has spent time in a steam room will immediately see the benefits to the skin. Moisture helps the skin to look fresh and dewy in the short term, but the benefits don't end there. A steam bath feels hotter than a sauna because the steam helps prevent sweat from evaporating and because humid air stores more heat than does dry air. In addition, when steam vapor hits the skin, it condenses with the sweat already on the skin to release what is known as the heat of condensation.

A sauna, on the other hand, has a low humidity so the body's core temperature stays cooler even though the temperature range is very high Fahrenheit.

Since both the sauna and the steam room provide benefits, the one that you choose is up to you. Both experiences are likely to help reduce stress and increase enjoyment of your gym or spa experience with regular use likely to produce the greatest rewards. Regardless of which you choose, using these rooms will create catharsis.

To decide which one is better, you may want to ask yourself: Is a steam room or a sauna best for me? Do I prefer dry heat or moist heat? Which facility am I likely to use on a regular basis?

If you are new to the sauna or steam room, start with short exposure and gradually increase the time you spend inside the rooms. These rooms are prevalent in Europe and Asia and home buyers in your area may be interested in this fixture. When they view this aspect, they will come with big money to buy your house. Be ready!

LIVING ROOM

Show Your Best Artwork

The word "living" in living room was used for living for 2,000 years until now. But now, even if a condominium or smaller home has a kitchen/living room combination, the name is used less frequently. And when there is a family room, homeowners tend to use the living room less often.

For all these centuries past, the living room was never called the "family room." It was just a room for the family to congregate. Once the family room (a.k.a.: "gathering room") popped up in 1965 in Dallas, Texas, the living room because less used to a point of not at all. In fact, all over the country, you will see more homes built without living rooms. If homes have a living room, it will be much smaller—about the size of a second bedroom, as compared with when it was the size of the master bedroom and most times larger, prior to 1965.

Many middle class homes built after the war had their entry door open directly into the living room. Today, the living room is further reduced by an entry hall, also called a "foyer." The foyer offers the homeowner more privacy and is cooler in design.

Keeping the living room will allow you to greet guests, formally, without them going into the main part of your house. By walking into a hall, you have one extra room with the same area, without having to walk through a room to get to the main part of the house.

The difference between a living room and a family room is access to the kitchen. If there is a wall and opening between the kitchen and where the family congregate, it's absolutely a living room. Modern living rooms never have never had a connection to

66

the kitchen. If the family and guests are in the direct sight of the kitchen, it's a family room.

Since 1965, architects have struggled with these two similar rooms. The solution: If there is to be a living room that no one will use, then make it smaller, or a more drastic approach would be to eliminate the living room altogether. The reasoning behind that is why put footage in a room if it is not used?

Show Your Best Furniture

Stop the train! You are remodeling and the living room is already there and you want to add on to another part of the house, not connected to your existing living room. The answer is to leave the living room with its fireplace and expand the entry, taking space away from the living room. Living rooms are great for holiday decorations since most face the street. This is the perfect place to put in a staircase—but only if you have another level. Da!

A Discerning Person

If you have a living room, consider using it for the following:

1. Show your best artwork.
2. Show your best furniture.
3. Play your piano.
4. Install surround sound speakers. (You may have guests who will enjoy surround sound music. Where better to sit and listen than in the living room?)
5. Receiving guests who you don't want entering your main house (i.e. IRS agents).
6. Overflow of guests at your large party. You will find the older folks will gravitate to the living room.

Most older homes have a wood burning fireplace. Until 1960, the fireplace in the living room was the only one in the house. Time to upgrade with gas and a remote turn on, if possible. Gas can be used to light wood burning logs or artificial logs. If you choose wood burning, be sure to have a spark arrester (screen at the top of the chimney).

The surround is what you can see in your room which goes around the fireplace unit and most surrounds are brick. Time to upgrade. The components of the surround are the tile stone around the unit, wood molding around the tile or stone, a mantle of either wood or stone, and the hearth to be on floor level to match surround. Put in a hearth whether you have a hardwood or tile floor and use the same hearth material as your mantle.

Most fireplaces are brick, either natural or painted. Time to upgrade to stone or tile surround (12" above the opening and 6" minimum on both sides with the hearth at 18"). If you have a tile floor, then no hearth is required, but it sure looks better.

The family room faces the rear yard while the living room faces the front of the house. It should be street facing and as attractive as you are able to afford. Visit leaded glass or grids (research) but no grids facing the rear yard.

Do not put a TV in the living room. Instead, put a mirror or a picture above the fireplace. Congratulations, you've evolved!

DINING ROOM

Where Your Guests Eat

The dining room has been around since the time of Babylon, but it has morphed from an open room to a closed-off room, from the kitchen with a door, sometimes double swinging. Back when the table was open to the fireplace and sleeping area, this was called a one-room house. Someone came up with the thought about building interior walls. This improved living conditions immensely.

The author cannot come up with the exact figures but coming close 20% of the world's population are still living without interior walls; some are living in a converted garage with only a bathroom and two walls.

Then along came the developer. The developer only built multiple homes that would sell. Hundreds of development projects sprang up after the war and continue today. What the developers did was to plan houses that were better than the previous. Constantly improving, they had an insight of what was better than those previously built, based on past sales.

The dining room is one of three sections of the house that can be called a room or an area. The dining room, closed off with walls and doors only, is a true dining room. If the table is open to other rooms, it's a dining area. The other is a breakfast area and sometimes sitting room, although a sitting room near the kitchen is not used in the modern home.

A dining area is not in the cards unless you have no other choice. When you walk into your house, the dining room should be next to the entry but accessible primarily from the kitchen. Open glass doors visible from the entry are acceptable and sometimes advisable since the dining room is a showcase for a beautiful table. The dining room should not be a direct part of the entry. An opening without doors may be in order. Your choice.

Windows Should Be Attractive

If you can afford one window in your dining room, then it should face the front of the house. No exceptions here. More than one window is okay as long as you still have wall space for furniture.

The second window can be three feet above the floor to allow a furniture piece. One table (extendable if need be), a buffet or sideboard, and of course, a plant. The buffet should have your better serveware and drawers for linens and silver flatware. Put the furnishings in the dining room but realize that each seat takes up two feet. Do not crowd the room with furniture. You should allow a minimum of a 3'– 6' distance from the table for cabinets or walls. Only a center chandelier with a dimmer is necessary.

Wallpaper, according to Joanna Gaines, is coming back. Install wallpaper or paint the walls so your pictures stand out without the distraction of wallpaper. One fixture in the center of the room should be lighted to allow guests to see what they are eating. Candles will do the rest.

The chandelier: People visiting Pottery Barn always ask the proper height above the table. It is 33" from the bottom of the table (tables are 30" tall). If the ceiling is more than 8" high, then raise the fixture 3" for every foot of ceiling height. Thus, if the ceiling is 10', then install a fixture 69" from the floor.

Author's note: As with living rooms, the dining room is going out. It still will be part of larger homes and especially home-owners who entertain. You should give valuable space for the largest rooms—possibly the kitchen and family room. The living room and dining room layout comes after you have that space already laid out. For smaller homes, consider a living room/dining room combination.

HOME OFFICE

Skip Traffic and Work from Home

Seven decades ago, there were no home offices, only a study and/or library. Some homes had a drawing room which served for reception or a place for ceremonies. After dinner, men would go directly to the drawing room to smoke cigars and talk politics. This room was situated near the front entrance since it was also used to greet business associates.

For decades, there were three types of people invited to enter the house.

First, the friends and relatives. They would go directly into the main part of the house.

Second were the guests or employees, such as the gardener and other employees who would come into the drawing room to receive payment for work that was done.

Third were the business people, such as a lawyer or someone to discuss a business transaction. They would be led into the study, which is now the office.

Guests would walk into the entry and go directly to the office, often to meet the householder. Many times, the guest would leave by the same route and out the front door without traversing the main part of the house or through a separate exterior door.

The drawing room morphed into the living room in modern times as it was situated near the entry. Times have changed and the living room is no longer a reception room. In fact, more, smaller homes are now being built without a living room.

The library was first introduced by architects about the time of the British castles. The thought, back then, was to have a serene place to read. Reading, from the time of Christ up until around 1948, was a favorite, albeit the only, pastime for adults. This ended with the invention of the television. There was still a library, but it morphed into a "study." The study took the prize for the shortest consistently-used room ever. The study was a room for writing. Beethoven wrote songs in his study. In fact, he spent almost half of his life in his study writing and composing music. If you walked into his study, you would think it was a library. The library/study was the thing for a short time, from Beethoven until 1956 when the home office showed up in developments in the Highlands section of Dallas, Texas. This led to a trend in home offices, nationwide.

Nearly every house featured a home office and the homes sold so fast that they had to be sold by a lottery system. If you were lucky, you got to buy one. It's called "flying off the market."

In all fairness, the home office was not the only reason the homes sold but it was one BIG reason. So now, this author has piqued your interest for an office. What to do next?

Design an office into your plan, but you have little space. What to do? Simple; plan a small room. The room need not be large. Only 100 square feet would be acceptable, larger if more space is available.

The location should be at the front of the house with an exterior door. This is ideal in order to conduct business without disturbing the household. The location, also near the entry, used to be the study. This exterior door also worked well when a quick exit to your car was important.

Today, the office is an integral part of the house since so many adults' work is done at home. The majority of CEOs use home offices to conduct business. Some do not go into the office building unless they need to for meetings. Who or what can be thanked for this innovation? The internet. The office today is filled with electronic devices used to conduct business remotely. It is seldom used today to receive associates.

Professionals need the office to conduct ongoing paperwork outside the workplace. This holds true for most professionals including the stay-at-home parent. The sitting room, next to the bedroom, can accommodate some of this work, but it is not suitable as a separate office.

Benjamin Franklin worked by candlelight. You need a well-lit LED desk and/or work area. The desk chair used to face the entry door of the office, but today it is preferred to have the desk chair facing the window. Put remote controlled blinds up and purchase the rapid-moving type since you may adjust many times during the day and night.

The bottom line for you is resale. Design an office and you will appeal to those very people who can afford your house.

A homeless guy, sprawled out on his cardboard box, speaking into his cell phone says, "Actually, I work from home."

THE ENTRY

Create a Good First Impression

Many brush off the entry as an afterthought, but it really is the first impression of your house when your guests walk into a nice entry. They instantly get the feeling that this is a good house.

In the 20th century, the architects treated the entry as only a front to enter the house. Times have changed since this misconception. Today, architects want a more grand entry. But we are the middle class; we don't want a grand entry—we want a proper entry.

First and foremost, the front door must reflect both you, as the homeowner, and the architectural style of your house. But of these two choices, choose what you prefer and design it. Yes, the front door is the first impression, but what you want for the guests next is a good second impression.

This author has seen many mid-century homes improved with a bundle of money without addressing the entry. The problem with most architects, and they will admit it, is that they draw lines the owner requests thinking—wrongly—that they are giving them what they desire. Let's stop. What would you rather have: the stamp of approval by you or someone who dares to suggest something else for your consideration? You may prefer a rose when others prefer a dandelion. I say, take the rose.

You may think you have no space to put in a bigger and better entry but that is not always true. The answer is to take unused space from the living room. Think of this: During the entire last month in your house, no one has used your living room except an IRS agent. It's time to wake up about how you are using your space. This is a major issue! The bottom line is to make the entry leading directly to the main part of your house as large as possible.

Should you put a guest closet in the entry? Answer: No. Period! This may come as a shock to many architects, but do they experience the crowd waiting to enter your home, while standing outside in the rain, waiting for other guests' coats and jackets to be hung? Not a way to go.

Put the guest closet somewhat away from the entry so all guests waiting to hang cloaks will be under the roof and not waiting outside in the rain. If your guests remove shoes, then you need to make accommodations for that, too. Have a small seat at the entry with shoe storage, below. The bottom line is to be considerate to your guests.

Aforementioned, the entry makes the first impression, so make it look nice and inviting, much like the rest of your house. Additional items to add to the entry may include a hanging light in the center of the ceiling, a grandfather clock, curio cabinet, and an umbrella stand. Grandfather clocks and curio cabinets lost favor in the 1980s but show off these items in your entry for an alluring first impression. Don't forget flowers or a potted plant.

The entry door should be an expression of yourself. This author feels that a nice entry door reflects a nice person. The challenge is on for you. This doesn't mean extravagant, it means proper.

Sometimes, the entrance of a one-story house opens directly into the living room. Let's design an entry that is not part of any room, just a small room, itself. This foyer should lead you to the living room to one side, and the dining room to the opposite side, then go directly into the main part of the house. If you have a second-story plan, this is where you put the staircase: in the entry.

This is not the place for a skylight; it's the place for a chandelier or any hanging light called a pendant. The foyer is the first impression for your guests and the chandelier is a reflection of you. Here's a suggestion: Put the chandeliers in a dome or coffered ceiling. Make the first impression as good as you can. Impress your visitors? Absolutely.

Beyond the foyer is the hallway which leads to the other parts of your house. Straight ahead you may enter the family room. Developers put rooms at the end of the foyer, such as the kitchen or family room. You can put these or any rooms there as long as there is a room. Best for the foyer is to lead to the main hallway.

GARAGE

Recharged Time

The garage in 1,000 BC was known as a carriage house. The door swung open on hinges and the horse would be backed into that space. When the carriage was completely inside, the horse would be unhooked and left in the stables to be cared for with feed and water in a corral.

Carriage doors primarily swung out and latched. While a lock was installed, it was seldom used—stealing a carriage was not an easy crime as it required a horse. Seeing two men running down the road with a carriage looked very suspicious, and if caught, they would be hanged.

Even during the time of wars, neither side would steal a carriage since that type of vehicle was not used on the battlefield, except in Ancient Rome when battles were fought with chariots.

During the mid-century, stealing a car was a profitable crime as there were no security devices—except to remove the key. Motor vehicle departments at that time just instituted prevention documents. Stealing an auto was directly related to the owners' laxity of leaving the key in the ignition when it was parked. Or, it could also be attributed to the ability of the thief to hot-wire the starter. A good thief could hot-wire the ignition in thirty seconds. Back then, your vehicle did not have a fighting chance.

This author once had his truck stolen. When he called the insurance agent on Monday to report it, the agent affirmed that he could see the "stolen vehicle" out his office window as it was parked directly across the street from his office. Of all the coincidences that could happen in one's life, this was, by far, number one. The truck was easy to recognize since his name and phone number were emblazoned on the door. Most likely, the truck was stolen by kids looking for a joyride since it was new, rather than a hardcore thief.

Don't Be Left Out

While on the subject of security, there is no better place to secure your car than in a garage. Most homes have a two-car garage; some have a one-car garage due to the lack of space on the lot for a larger garage. After all, when the house was built, who thought families would own two automobiles?

Today, the two-car garage is the norm for this country. Now the question in your design is where to place the garage? If you have a corner lot, put it on the side not facing the front door. If you do not have a corner lot, put it in the front. Da!

During the mid-century and following the war, a majority of garages were detached with an eight-foot-wide driveway from the street to the rear of the lot where the garage was located. This took up lots of valuable property.

Do you know how many homeowners have asked how to get the garage to be part of the house in order to have a bigger yard? Too many.

The problem is that there is a regulated minimum distance width called a "side yard setback." More and more, the departments are calling for five-foot setbacks between the property line and the house. This is based on a fire code for firefighters to have access to the back of the house. Because of this difficulty, tearing down and rebuilding a house with an attached garage came about. Tear it down and put the garage where you wish and satisfy the restrictions at City Hall.

If your garage is detached, don't forget the umbrella. If your garage is attached, then your resale value increases immensely. Ideally, a garage door should lead directly into the kitchen. This makes unloading the groceries convenient.

Let's return to the doors. You can be creative and have sliding doors as barn doors or have swinging doors if your space allows. Or, you can install overhead sectional doors.

This author accepts the fact that things will change, especially in the design and construction of homes. However, one item that will remain far into the future is the overhead sectional door. There are multiple styles to choose from to fit the architecture of your house, from traditional to modern.

So what about the flooring? Concrete is what is used for garage flooring. Your house may have a raised floor with a crawl space underneath, but the garage floor has always been concrete. Since you want your garage floor to look good, here are some options:

Place to Get Recharged

The easiest and most cost effective way to improve the look of your concrete garage floor is to paint it. A dark grey will improve the concrete look but not by much. If you paint the garage floor, look into using a color not too light to reveal dirt and tire marks, but also not too dark to show water marks. Caution: Let the paint dry for three to four days before parking your vehicle on it, then drive into the newly-painted garage slowly.

The next evolution in concrete is epoxy. Epoxy is so durable, it will outlast paint by twenty years. It is available at most home suppliers. To apply epoxy, first roll on the epoxy in the color of your choice (you can add speckles to this, also available at your home supply store).

This method is mostly done by professionals, but you can do it yourself. The key is to spread the epoxy on a small area at a time, then add the speckles as you go. Once you get it going, the task is not that difficult. Don't skimp on the speckles. When using speckles, it is best to have one person do the whole floor so that the technique will be consistent. After about a week, apply a coat of sealant.

Sometimes, a washer and/or dryer is in the garage. Take it out, put it somewhere else, even if it is in the hall. If you don't have much space for storage, then put in a stackable unit which only requires 9-square feet, maximum.

The tank water heater in your garage must go. Period. Unless it is a tankless heater, then a corner of the garage is a good location.

Provide for an electrical hook-up for rechargeable cars. This is the time to meet with your electrical contractor. You need a minimum of 200 amps, and if your house is larger, then 400 amps are necessary. Check with your city power department about this. Think about the houses built with a one-car garage. If they only knew they could have read this book! Don't make the same mistake. Put in provisions for two chargers. Don't be left out.

This author once took the family touring in a rented motor home. It was lots of fun. Leaving the KOA facilities to go back home, one of the kids yelled, "Where is Danny?" After a quick turnaround to the camp, we found Danny standing in the spot we had occupied. Don't be left out!

A larger service may be required for a recharger for your car. The bottom line is that every garage should have provisions for a rechargeable car. The future is here. Even Harley Davidson has come out with a rechargeable motorcycle.

Follow the Guidelines

Today's garage is insulated and drywalled with a small heat pump in the wall for heat and air in the event that you may want to work on your car. Ha!

This author has a three-year-old car and only twice has the hood been open. Even changing the oil is time consuming work of the past. Some car washes provide a free car wash with an oil change. This author is an authoritarian when it comes to homes, but knows very little about cars. My questions remain: Why synthetic oil is so expensive and why one must use high octane gas when 82-octane will work 100% of the time for new cars and small trucks? A book could be written about these misconceptions, but let's stick to the subject of your house.

Besides the sectional overhead door, there is to be an entry door either leading into the house and/or an exterior door to the yard or side of the house. The door can have a window, preferably with blinds between the glass. (These windows can be found at your home center.) A window should be at least 12 square feet (that's 4' x 3') or as large as 16 square feet, but no larger, since you will prefer wall space. The window can be non-operable since ventilation is not a concern.

A well-planned garage has provisions for storage, such as gardening equipment. Even larger houses cannot afford this luxury elsewhere on the property, therefore, it goes in the garage. Most garages today have space for two cars as required by code. It's best to park two cars in your two-car garage. But what about the gardening equipment? Simply make the garage two feet deeper and two feet wider, at a minimum. This will also give you more ingress to your car doors.

For lighting, this is one part of the house with no canister lights. Put in a minimum of six 24" florescent lights, flush with the ceiling. The space will light up beautifully, look good, and be energy-efficient.

Install a few wall outlets for work stations, 48" above the floor. With your garage as nice as this, you are ready for a major party, such as a wedding or house warming. For this purpose, your caterer will use your garage to unload all their fodder and their tables. Also, during a party, a ping pong table can be set up there temporarily.

This author allows filmmakers to use the garage as central control while filming in other parts of the house. They actually bring their own desks, tables, and equipment for the duration of the filming and leave the garage cleaner than ever.

Since you are building another two feet wider than department minimum requirements, you have the space for a tankless water heater. In addition to using a tankless washer for everyday use, the author's wife keeps an older washer in the corner for washing dirty rages and such. Those previously hung out on a clothesline. Ha! My guess is it would be difficult to find clothes pins these days. Oh, have time changed! But clothes pins are still manufactured today. Stay with it and you will find what you are looking for.

HALLWAYS AND FOYERS

No Detours

Post-war, all hallways were 42" wide to accommodate a door at the end with 3.5-inch casings (the molding on both sides and the top of door openings) to fit nicely on all sides. This hall size was the norm until 1975, when, due to cost constraints, the halls were reduced to 36" wide and the casings were reduced in size to 1 3/8", also for cost savings.

The 36" hall remained popular for 30 years. In 2005, hall width returned to 42", partly because the casings became wider (2 ½") and the 42" hall was more easily passable. (I'm not saying people got wide—no, not me!)

Today, there is more traffic in the halls due to the powder room and built-in linen closets. Also, homeowners are using the halls once again for displaying art work and family pictures in wall galleries. Halls are a necessity, but keep in mind: the fewer halls, the better. They add to the construction footage but do zero for the size of the affected rooms.

When planning a second floor, be sure the head (top) of the stairs is a foyer and not a hall. You never want the head of the stairs to lead directly into a wall. An open foyer space does not have to be large. Once at the head of the stairs, you enter a foyer which leads to the bedrooms on both sides. No hall—just a foyer. Only your architect knows!

Of course, this means the stairs must be in the center of the house and center of the upstairs bedroom. The foyer should have at least one large window. If a window is not possible, then put in a skylight. This is one of the few times a skylight is recommended.

This author frowns on skylights, except in the second-floor foyer where you need natural light.

The first-floor foyer does not need a skylight since the front door may be glass to let in light or a solid front door with a side, tall narrow window called a side light. The foyer on the second floor can also be used for a small study for the kids. Generally, it's a quiet place with no TV, no music, and no refrigerator—no fun! Don't know who said it, but the children who study in a study become studious.

Motion Lights

Light the main hallway with 6" LED recess lights if the width is 42", but if the hallway is wider, place wall sconces every 12' along the wall. Matching ceiling lights should come on with two switches and dimmers. Additionally, a portion of the hall can have a motion light for convenience.

Motion lights can be life saving. Walking into a room to first switch on a light in the dark may be very hazardous and deadly if you trip and hit your head. Put in motion lights everywhere, even if you set them for five seconds. Five seconds could save your life, especially if your bedrooms are on a second floor. The location of the stairs in the dark may not be found by the one walking in the dark. Don't take a chance.

Put a motion light in the walk-in pantry, walk-in closet, walking into the garage outside each rear door, every hallway, powder room and anywhere you want. This light can be switched off from inside or hardwired to bypass the switch. You can have both. Do it right.

GUEST BATH & GUEST COAT CLOSET

Thoughtfulness

We all have guests knocking on the door. Sometimes they only want to chat or they expect you to invite them out to dinner, unless you are prepared to have them stay for dinner. But if it's your rich uncle, you will want to make points in favor of inheritance, so consider a guest room. Whether it's a rich uncle or a close friend or relative, be prepared with your remodeling or new construction to plan the best accommodation for them.

The bedroom should have its own bath with a shower. The bathroom should have paper towels, no hanging cloth towels. You want them to feel germ free. Be sure the closet is cleared of your storage items. Also, you might want to have a bedside clock and TV on the wall with a remote. Think of this accommodation as you would a hotel, with plenty of bath towels. Don't forget the tissue paper and assortment of plants in the bedrooms and bath. We have mentioned first impressions. Here, you want to give a lasting impression.

It's a good idea to have one of these rooms available for your rich uncle. It can be an occupied room and quickly converted to a guest room. Thus, the advantage of an extra bedroom.

The guest bath, also known as the powder room, is to be located in the center of your house, accessible, but not visible, from the family room. You don't need a shower. Guests use the shower in the bath adjoining or nearest to the guest room.

There should be limited or no cabinets and a pedestal sink. Be absolutely sure the toilet cannot be viewed from outside of the powder room when the door is open.

The ventilating fan comes on with the light switch. One switch is for lights and a fan—one switch. The *number one* objective of every American homeowner is to be able to turn on the light without the ventilating fan because they think the fan is an added electrical cost, but the fan prevents mold and odor. Not having it this way is penny wise, pound foolish!

A good location for a powder room is off a hall but not off the entry. The entry location went out with the turn of the century. Be realistic. You walk into the house and your first impression is a toilet room. Case closed. Install a double paper holder and loose paper hand towels. There should be no towel bars and no racks. It is not proper to have guests using the same hanging towel.

Attention to Detail

The inside of the door should have a partial or full-height mirror. Your guests will appreciate your thoughtfulness. Also, a picture-framed mirror above the sink. No medicine cabinet. Remember, this is a very short-visit room to tidy up.

The coat closet, also known as a guest closet, was formerly located in the entry. This location had been around for decades but no more. A good location is near the powder room or in a hall.

Even if you don't entertain much, the location of these smaller rooms is a convenience for your family. A shoe closet and a chair or bench at the entry is also a thoughtful choice with more homeowners and guests removing their shoes. This should be in an inconspicuous location, such as under the stairs with the bench outside of the closet. The coat closet will be used for the family's additional hanging clothes. But free up some space for a large party by removing your stored items. Be a discerning homeowner. You are remodeling the middle-class home. Think outside the box!

BATHS # 2 AND 3
Sustainable Design

Baths number two and three can be identical or completely different. Neither require a tub. A shower is for safety. The main shower head is to be plumbed 6' 6" from the shower floor.

Put in at least one handicap shower without a shower dam that gives you the ability to roll in a wheelchair; it should have one or two grab bars and a seat. A handicap shower is good for all ages. The guidelines are called ADA, Americans with Disabilities Act.

In common use today are the combination shower head and hand-held shower. The shower head can be used for a regular shower or removed for a hand-held. This set up is used extensively in Europe and the Middle East.

Install an exhaust fan with a built-in light and one recess light nearest the shower and toilet. Use wall sconces above and to the side of the wall hung mirror. Exhaust fans are available with a heating-light feature. Research.

Even if two people share this bath, it's okay to have one basin. The votes are in: It is a winner to have more counter space rather than two basins. Unfortunately, there is generally not room to put the toilet in a compartment, but a dividing wall would be considerate. The vanity cabinet should have at least four drawers for more than one person to store their personal items.

Install a two-bulb ceiling heater with a separate switch or a heater with a ventilating fan. This is great for drying after coming out of the shower and it lights up the entire room. Be sure the ceiling heat register (the vent where heat comes into the room from your heating system) is at least 24" from this ceiling heater to not diminish the effectiveness of the heater.

Be cognizant of the use of switches. You can use one switch for everything to come on at the same time but this is never done. This author challenges someone to go into the bath and turn on one switch. The reason this is not done is because if only one switch is turned on and another item is wanted, it provides the option to return to the other switches. After one time, this will not happen. Therefore, install as few switches as possible.

The shower should have a shampoo niche, generally located on the same wall as the shower head. This prevents water from splashing in. A soap dish is necessary unless the shampoo shelf will double up. You can also put in a soap dish if the bath is to be used by more than one person. You can also install a low ledge for those who want to shave their legs.

This Makes Life Simple

Only use ½" frameless glass shower doors. Today, the shower glass is self-cleaning. It costs more, but it looks good for the appraiser and it is clean.

Shower curtains are still in vogue. Curtains are easy to manipulate, cost less, and can be easily changed. They are also good for privacy.

Then there is the shower without doors or curtains. This must be a minimum of 25 square feet or larger and the bath floor must be tiled to the shower, which is often done. In this size shower, you can put in two seats.

The advantage of a large shower is that you don't need a shower door. The disadvantage is that it is not very warm and you cannot create a steam feeling. Of course, you can have a large shower and shower doors which means less upkeep on the glass. Again, the glass does come self cleaning.

Another bath is the Jack and Jill bath (a bath utilized by two bedrooms) but it does not fit in with today's scheme of things. Stop to note the term "Jack and Jill" which is not politically correct. I guess it is open to your interpretation.

It is always best to have a separate bath for each bedroom. Stay away from a hall bath (mid-century). You don't want your family and guests having to go from the bath to their bedroom by using a common hallway. If you have a smaller house, all this could change. The objective is to plan for the best bath arrangement as the area will allow, then cut back to what will fit best. When it comes down to resale value, at least you have covered the bases.

Enjoying What Your House Has to Offer

Also to consider is the linen. Towel bars are used less. Towel shelves above the toilet are a good place to put folded towels on a metal rack. One hand-towel rack will be sufficient if it holds two hand towels or better to have loose paper towels laid on the counter. A towel bar on the shower door is also good for convenience. A towel bar can double as a handle to open the door.

Make provisions for a weighing scale. The scale can be anywhere on the floor or slide under the vanity to be used as needed.

In terms of the toilet, the best toilets are elongated with a soft-closing lid. Standard size toilets are out. Period.

One thing that is a must in every bathroom is a window (except for the powder room) where the ventilation required is only one-and-a-half square feet—but you will want more.

The average window in a secondary bath is six square feet, with three operable square feet. You don't care since you have ventilating fans which are much better since the air changes every five minutes. But it's the natural light from the window.

Build it Better

Mirrors have changed over the last century. A mirror cemented to the wall is out. You want picture-framed mirrors to conform to your style house. You can also get picture-framed mirrors with built-in lights and switches on the mirror. It looks and works great. Research.

Since 1955, designers have come up with innovated tile for shower walls and bath floors. This author was caught up in this phenomenon. Tile on walls were: 4" x 4", 6" x 6", and 12" x 12". Tile floors were 12" x 12" or 2" x 2". Don't overlook subway tile on walls, which is a classic look.

Let's be real. Anything tiled properly looks good if it is in the best interest of your house. When you take a shower, do you give any attention to the tile? You do not. The attention is when you view the tile from outside and are not taking a shower. What is correct tile? None of the above.

This author suggests you close this book and visualize the proper tile. Ready? Close this book. Okay, you can open this book and are you right? Proper tile on the shower is subway tile. This is tile of the same size, staggered. Subway tile has been seen in New York and Chicago train stations from their inception. This is the tile layout you must use since it is timeless. Subway tile is available everywhere, in sizes from small to large, from grouted to non-grouted. The bottom line, use subway tile in your shower. Become timeless! Use subway tile for the walls of the shower, but use more updated tile for the shower floor. Here, the smallest tile is the best for no slippage. Tile comes in square-foot sheets. This is the best for you. It is non-slip, which is best with the soap dropping. This tile comes in regular and glass. Either is fine. Caution: Do not use pebble-stone tile on floors. It's hard on the feet.

Your bath floor can be 12" x 12" or 2" x 2", depending on the décor. Bath floors do not have a slippery condition since you should use a floor mat when stepping out of the shower. Therefore, any bath floor tile will be acceptable.

The counter tops are to be stone with a backsplash of 5" stone or tile, the same as the shower floor with a tile border. No matter what style your house, follow these suggestions. You can't go wrong. It's not where you look but what to look for.

MEDIA CENTER / RECREATION ROOM
Drinks Are Served

In 1928, the first media room was designed into the upper class homes. They were elaborate with individual movie seats facing the screen. The screen was a white roll-down, much like a large shade. The projector was a machine with 1" film with perforations to fit around spoke wheels, and a small light bulb aimed at the screen. The projectionist took a film disc and threaded it through the projector. A small motor moved the tape to pass the bulb, thusly showing images on the white screen.

The projectionist had to be careful not to allow the machine to stop at any time since it would melt the film and the tape would have to be spliced on a splicing machine, flat on a tabletop.

This was a great way to entertain guests since many did not have this setup and, of course, drinks were served.

In 1940, there were about 1,500 of these media centers in our country. The two movies *Gone with the Wind* and *The Wizard of Oz* were big hits. Friends knew of these showings and the viewing rooms were packed, even though most had seen the movies a year earlier at the theater.

At the same time, this room was also called the recreation room and most were in the basement or, in larger homes, on the third floor. For this showing, a very large projector was used to hold the film. The movies were in two or three segments, which allowed guests to take a break while the reel was rewound and the next segment set to show.

Of course, drinks were served but not from the media room. They were brought in by servants. Generally, this gathering was on a Sunday afternoon after an early dinner.

The media room was a "must" for executives in the entertainment business. Of the 1,500 installations, about 1,000 were in and around Hollywood, California. But as word spread, every wealthy person building a new house began to factor in a media room, each outdoing the other with more elaborate décor. You would try not to get a seat at the back of the room next to the projector since it was somewhat noisy. The sound for the movie came from the projector.

This high-style media room lasted for 40 years, a lifetime in our modern age of electronics. Then, in 1970, along came "Mad Man Muntz" as he called himself in his advertisements. His television projected the show on a much bigger screen: as large as 4' x 3'. But Muntz went out of business in 1995 due to the innovation that changed the lifestyle of home living—as well as remodeling—the flat screen TV.

The Object in Life is to Play

Prior to 2005, there were flat screen TVs but the cost was above the average homeowners' pocketbook. Today, how large is the wide screen TV? Well let's take a look at the Dallas Cowboy stadium. This screen is almost as large as their football field. You can watch a replay ten times bigger than life.

If you get a room on the Las Vegas Strip, your view of digital signage is breathtaking and they are continuously becoming bigger and better.

This brings us back to the media center in our little ol' house. With the innovation of the flat screen came media centers in middle-class homes. Although not as elaborate as those rich folks', it was nice enough to impress your friends. Flat screens that cost thousands became available for hundreds of dollars. In 1952, the television weighed 122 pounds. Today, the flat screen TV weighs an average of 19 pounds.

Feeling Good About Your Dreams

You must have space for a media room. Generally, it takes as much space as a family room, unless you are the CEO of Warner Brothers. He has an entire lower floor of his California house as a media center. He lives directly across the street from this author who has yet to receive an invitation to sit in his media room. I guess it's a separation of upper class and middle class divided by the side of the street. Maybe that will change when he reads this book.

The media room is the very last room to plan when planning your house. You do not want to plan around a media center. The seating arrangement hasn't changed in almost a century but friendlier accommodations can be added, like a bar where drinks are served. Situate the bar, no matter how small it is, at the rear of the room with a bar sink. Guests can mix their own drinks as compared to a century ago when the drinks were delivered as ordered. Acculturate to life today in the USA!

Going Beyond

Now that you have planned a media room, if your friends are not watching movies that they have seen before, or are not into watching movies at all, you can use it as your recreation room. Can't find your son? Check the media room or recreation room. Videos are now taking over the space reserved for movies, and drinks are not served.

The recreation room came long before the media center. Hundreds of years ago, the French and English put recreation rooms in all of their castles. Ballrooms? The author is open to feedback.

Okay, so you say your house is your castle. And you have space for a rec room, then think about how you will use it. What really goes into a rec room? Not a fireplace. This is not for intimacy. The number one item going in the rec room is the pool table, followed by a slot machine, TV, small walk-up bar (which could be a juice bar), a card table, fish tank, sports pictures or paintings, and anything to do with people in motion. Lots of plants. Bring the outdoors in.

WINE CELLAR
More Drinks Are Served

The term "wine cellar" has been used incorrectly for a long time. If you go downstairs to a wine cellar, then it is a wine cellar. But if it is in a room, then it is a wine room or a wine vault.

Regardless of what it is called, this room is placed near the kitchen for no other reason than it has always been. The wine cellar first came about when glass bottles were invented about the year 1000 BC Back then, in order to keep temperatures at 55 degrees Fahrenheit, it had to be underground and insulated with heavy timber ceilings and stone walls. When the master of the house wanted a particular wine, the servant went to the cellar to retrieve it—and fast. Therefore, this author wonders why the wine cellar wasn't placed near the dining room and not in the kitchen.

Most homes cannot afford the luxury of a true cellar so a wine vault is the choice. Today, we have a luxury not available hundreds of years ago: temperature control. A simple temperature control device of 55 degrees can be installed in any room. But it's better to start with insulated walls, not weather-insulated walls but temperature-insulated walls and ceiling.

This author has stepped into dozens of wine rooms and noticed they all have something in common, not all racks were full, and most were not 60% full. And there were few or no tables. These were large wine rooms with space for 1,000 bottles but no tables. Is it that this author is too much of a romanticist? Probably not.

So let's design a wine room that this author has never seen. Walk into the room and see racks with wine—a given. Then what? The focal point should be tile mosaic or painting of a wine item, such as a vineyard or bottles of wine. This should be about 12 square feet, minimum. A motion light lights the room and the mosaic, brightly. There are closed cabinets for boxes and a table with two to four chairs with a light above (chandelier or other pendant light). The table can be as small as 24 inches.

It is better to have a table and mosaic than to have a bigger wine display. To see so many open racks does not look or feel good. It has the impression of your real true worth, especially to others. So what to do? Get inexpensive wine to fill the spaces (Trader Joes has wine for $3 a bottle.) As your better wine comes in, give away the cheaper wine. This author will take it.

The objective is to make your room, whether a cellar or a vault, look as nice and complete as possible. It's like keeping your car clean and shiny. Who cares? You do!

Going Beyond

The door to your wine room should be special. This door is to be the second best door in your house, next to the front door. The best choice would be wrought iron and glass. When your guests arrive, they will ask, "What's that?" You will tell them that it's your wine room. Then they get to see it. If it's proper, you will leave an everlasting impression on them since they won't have one—guaranteed!

Consider a dumbwaiter. A dumbwaiter is a small elevator for conveying wine from the cellar. It can be used to send food and other items to multiple floors. There are down sides though. Today, the mechanisms are somewhat noisy, some noisier than an elevator. It also takes up a lot of space, and in smaller homes this could be an issue as that space could also be used for closets. Additionally, the shaft collects insects. Even when tight doors are used, insects somehow find their way into that area. Sometimes, insects from the inside of the door will make their escape when you open it and the light streams in. To remedy this, keep the shaft sprayed and install a gas repellant, available at home centers.

The loading time should not be a factor. If the butler walks down the stairs and loads the dumbwaiter with one or two bottles, it adds to the ambience. You wait, all knowing the process of retrieving the bottles is part of the relaxing stage.

Let's now delve into the fantasy world of wine cellars.

From Ordinary to Extraordinary

Perhaps you have an upslope lot in the back of your yard. Dig out a 15' x 15' space for an underground but on level wine cellar. Put in a concrete block structure and cover it with soil on the top. In order words, you are building a wine shelter where temperature control is no problem. They'll be space for a table and two to four chairs and about 500 bottles of the wine of your choice. If you have a tree nearby, hang an exterior chandelier from it. Fantasy, yes! Reality—possible. And don't forget the glass and wrought-iron entry door.

If you build it, this author will come with a bottle of Dom Perignon. I'm only an email away.

There are upgrades to the upgrades. What goes good with wine? You guessed it—cheese. Some cheese can be stored in the cellar and lasts a long time. Put in a small refrigerator, either a door type or drawer. A small sink for cleaning glasses can be drained to the landscape outside. Music? A sound system with a disc player. How about the theme from *Days of Wine and Roses* or "Follow the Yellow Brick Road" from *The Wizard of Oz*. Okay, I guess the author has had too much wine.

BASEMENT

Come to Life

A cellar is not a basement. A cellar is primarily used for storage or for *a* wine cellar, whereas, a basement is a habitat area which may or may not include storage and/or a wine cellar.

Basements east of the Mississippi in the early 20th century were for storage of fuel oil and general storage. The city buildings were built three or four stories above ground and the basement, below ground. Access was from the front and the back stairs. The poorly-lit stairs were used to retrieve fuel oil. More than 35% of homes in the early 20th century had basements. They were dark and sometimes infested with rodents.

This changed with the movement out West. One-story homes were built without a basement. In fact, it wasn't until 1927 when the California basement became the rage. This was not a true basement but was an area for storage of the water heater and the heating unit. Access was a staircase, usually very precarious, to descend under the one- or two-story house. Rodents were not as prevalent since the outside vents prohibited intrusion. An interior door usually accessed the basement. Sometimes a double exterior door at ground level. Also known as a trap door.

This layout was prevalent in 70% of homes out West until the 60s. With the advent of concrete slab floors, designers put the mechanical devices elsewhere.

However, the basement allure continued and the builder/home-owners moved on past the concrete slab construction. Engineers designed concrete slab floors also to be the ceiling of the basement. Today, the basement, supported by exterior cinder-block walls, brings it back to life.

In some cities, the basement does not come into lot coverage. This is an advantage for those wanting to build larger homes on a smaller lot. This area can also be considered a recreation room, bonus room, media center, or a play room.

Economy or Luxury?

The ventilation is to be considered with a basement. There should always be a well at the level of your basement floor that leads up and allows for an escape route. A window or glass sliding door to a well should always be installed in case of emergency. The operable glass is at least 5% of the floor area.

The old basement with dangerous declining stairs must now have standard 36" wide standard staircases, in most cases, with oak wood and plenty of light. The basement can also include a media center and wine cellar. This is getting up in the world from the basement level!

The downside is the huge cost of constructing retaining walls on all sides and sealing those walls from water intrusion. If a bath is required, and it is below sewer level, a pump is in order. This pump is not a huge investment compared to the overall cost.

A well-designed, pest-free basement with a pool table and walk-up bar makes for better living. Build it and invite your friends.

SOLARIUM VS. CONSERVATORY

Accumulating Happiness

Just imagine your guests walking into this room and seeing the group of orchids, the topiary, and artifacts retrieved from around the world. You will definitely hear a "Wow!" This could be the legacy of your house.

Okay, so you don't travel to Hong Kong, instead you visit a swap meet. Why not? The objective here is to have fun and more fun.

There is one big factor in favor of this room: it's timeless. It will work in a modern, contemporary, or traditional house design and you can also give it a hint of English, French, or Asian style.

So you have a combination solarium and conservatory. What to call it?

Answer: This is your Sol-Con room. No need to take off your shoes.

Elsewhere in this book, the author describes a parlor where invited friends can play cards. Use the Sol-Con room, also at night, but be sure to serve tea!

Do you want to visit a special place? Do you want to see a conservatory that is the world's best? Go to Las Vegas to the Bellagio Hotel. There you will see a conservatory that they change six times a year. Breathtaking is the word to use. You will want to take more pictures there than any place you have previously visited—with your family in the foreground—and don't miss the living wall.

In the event that any Bellagio Hotel executives read this book, would they be so kind as to give this author a discounted rate on rooms? Probably that won't happen!

Living the Middle Class Dream in America

A solarium or conservatory leaps into the upper-class homes. England has many 20,000 square foot modern-day homes with a conservatory. The solarium has been primarily used to sit, have tea, and enjoy the sunlight, especially on cold or blustery days.

You can plan in a conservatory. No one has to say what size. It can be smaller, but not very small. Here, you can care for plants not able to survive outside in the mainland of the United States. The reason they survive here is lots of glass which keeps plants healthy and temperature-controlled. You are not cultivating many plants, just a few varieties for show. This is also great place to grow a small topiary. As you travel around the world, you will most likely find some décor item that will fit right in. You will need to design in two items:

First, an area to water down plants where the water will drain into the ground. Since you may incorporate a solarium, a floor drain would be in order.

Additionally, you need a hose bib (water faucet) with a retractable hose.

After you visualize your conservatory along one or two walls, leave space for the solarium. Both entities have something in common: glass, sunlight, and tranquility. For the most efficiency, this room should be facing south. A table and four chairs is all that is necessary to call this a solarium since you have the glass, both overhead and on two walls.

Put a circulating fan above the table with variable speeds. At the planning stage, use construction paint and paint on the floor to delineate the portion of the conservatory and the table location with exact dimensions of the fan above. Your FAU contractor will need to zone this room properly. The floor at the portion of the room not used for watering should be tiled. Recently, this tile has emerged from rustic to a 12" x 12" small, glass, clean-look porcelain.

FREESTANDING STRUCTURES

A Dream House

Freestanding means the structure is not connected to the main house. If it is a separate building with two or more structures, you are leading to call your property a "compound," especially if you also have a freestanding garage. Generally, this structure can't be incorporated into your house plan but added at a later date.

Say you build and/or remodel your house on a limited budget. After a few years, if space allows, you are able to add separate structures. Some will require a bath sewer line to connect to the existing house line. If you plan ahead by designing a master plan, then the sewer connection and water lines will be no worry.

The most popular freestanding structure is the pool house, followed by the guest house, gazebo, outdoor kitchen, covered spa, a second garage, workroom, and a conservatory. This author has not seen an aviary. Just a thought: You can make your backyard an aviary by keeping a supply of wild bird seed in a small plot near a tree. Control the number of birds by the amount of seeds you toss.

At present, this author is building a combination recreation room and office which is in the permit process. The plan is to build a 1,200-square-foot structure, separate from the main house. The existing orchard will have to be relocated, which means relocating mature trees. A weekend battle! The plan now is to scatter the trees to other locations on the lot. Planting and replanting fruit trees can be done any time of year in California, notwithstanding a frost.

Altogether, the recreation room will have a media center, a pool table, a sit-down bar, a wine room with space for 500 bottles, and an office. Notice the word "space." The author was given a five-cent slot machine in 1990 so there needs to be a recreation room for this slot machine. Okay, 1,200 square feet is a bit much, but there will be lines to use this machine, so I'm planning ahead. Need the money!

Speaking of money, you can rent out these freestanding structures, such as the guest house or even the garage. Some municipalities even allow for garage living. For this, you will need to drywall the walls and put in a heat pump which will give you heat and air conditioning for about 400 square feet of space. Also, you will need to insulate the walls, ceiling and garage door.

Leave the garage door in place in order to revert to the original purpose, if needed. A bath is necessary with a shower. It can be added outside since it is a small room. This could also be available for use by the workers.

Not to be overlooked is a combination freestanding building, such as a garage/pool house, open to your needs and budget. The upside is that freestanding structures definitely add lots of value to your property. The downside is that renting out a building at the rear of your lot requires space for parking and limits your privacy. But if it's a relative, you most likely can make it work.

GUEST HOUSE VS. POOL HOUSE

A Can-Do Spirit

Guest houses and pool houses have many department regulations. If you have a large lot, you will have fewer difficulties. But if you have a smaller lot, suitable for a pool/guest house, regulations apply but they can be overcome. Most officials will grant a pool house, even if you don't have a pool.

The pool house consists of a large room which can be used as a recreation room and a bath with a shower. This freestanding structure, approved anywhere in this country, has a big downside—there is no kitchen. You can have cabinets, a refrigerator, and microwave oven, as well as a bar sink, but no living facilities. This means, it would be difficult for someone to live in the pool house. This is the objective of the authorities; the pool house is for recreation, but not for living, especially for renting. This makes sense since that is all you want. Why would you want to rent out your pool house and have strangers on your property?

Renting out a pool house devalues the property even though it brings in income. The bottom line is that the income is small compared to what you will have to pay for your mortgage payments.

Let us set aside the rental aspect. The pool house, in itself, has good resale value. It adds square footage to your property. This is number one when it comes to selling.

The convenience of a pool house for family and guests is unlimited. Visit a friend's house with a pool house. You bring with you all of your pool attire. After the pool experience, you go into the pool house and take a shower, then get ready to party—or party first.

Additionally, the pool house bath can be used by caretakers and construction workers as you remodel. This shows your appreciation for others, which may return to you many times over by the workers' loyalty.

Happiness is Related to One's Efforts

A pool house is nice, but what you really want is a guest house. This may be attached to the main house or it may be a separate structure. A guest house typically is double the size of the pool house.

How valuable is the guest house? Answer: The most expensive houses in the country have guest houses.

Most building departments did not recognize guest houses until 1975. Prior to that time, illegal apartments were created. The departments needed to address this foreboding issue. How to legalize these units? They came up with the "guest house" and along came the state's mandate for guest houses. The state government mandates every city to provide a guest house. All the cities complied, but with a caveat that structures must meet each city's zoning code. The term today is ADU (Auxilliary Dwelling Unit).

The structure must meet some requirements, as with the main building, with proper lot coverage and setbacks, sometimes with a minimum one car off-street parking. Put this in the hands of your architect or take a scaled plan to the city department for pre-plan check, which costs nothing. You will be pleasantly surprised at how helpful they will be for you.

You ask, "What is a guest house?" Answer: A living area with bath and complete kitchen facilities.

A guest house is a perfect place to live while you are remodeling the main house. But the guest house does not necessarily have to be free standing. It can be attached to the main house as long as it has complete kitchen facilities with a separate entrance.

A guest house can be rented out and you can get more per square footage added to the main house for appraisal valuation. Oh, and of course, the guest house is ideal for guests. President Ford stayed in a guest house while visiting a friend in Rancho Santa Fe, California. He probably got a discount!

Most building departments don't require another garage or carport but they usually ask for off-street parking and sometimes require paving.

Make a Big Impact

A majority of guest houses in this country are one bedroom, one story. The ideal size is 650 square feet. If you have a two-story house, the departments will allow a guest house above the garage.

While designing a guest house, consider an outside bathroom for guests and gardeners. If you don't have a pool-house bath, then have it attached to the structure. A shower will seldom be used but an outside shower is a great hit with the kids. You can put the shower inside this room or put an outside shower in as long as the water drainage is proper.

Items to have in your guest house:

1. A fireplace—smaller, about 36" x 24".
2. Smaller dishwasher—a single-drawer type will work.
3. Microwave oven.
4. Drop in a two-burner cook top—no hood.
5. Smaller window over the sink, facing the yard.
6. Shower—make it large, 5' x 5' but no shower door is needed.

7. Vanity with two sinks, with picture framed mirrors.

8. Washer and dryer—stackable and gas, if available.

9. TV above the fireplace and one opposite the bed. Pretend you are in a high-end suite at Caesars Palace on vacation.

10. Motion light to come on when you enter at night. Set for five to ten seconds. This is enough time to set and turn on the wall switch or to pass through the bedroom or bathroom. It is best to set it to come on only when it is very dark. Follow directions.

PATIOS AND MORE

Living the Middle-Class Dream in America

Patios have been around since the beginning of house construction, dating back to ancient China. Every house built during the last 500 years had a rear yard. The yard had two sections: the landscape and the patio where the family would sit privately and enjoy conversation and drink tea.

The exception, of course, was no backyard. Less than 5% of American homes have no backyard. These few homes may enjoy a side or front yard, generally with a porch. We are speaking of single-family homes, not apartments. Most municipalities require at least a 15-foot rear yard to be maintained.

All this, most likely, does not come into play for your house. This author is not addressing buildings to cover most of the lot, so let's move on.

The patio can be open landscape or covered. It can be covered with solid or open-spaced material and attached to the main house. The covered patio, which lends itself to good resale value but is more costly, should be structurally built to withstand the elements.

The covered patio was first introduced in America in 1915. The structure was built with whatever the builder thought would hold up, generally covered with tin, and in later years, corrugated fiber glass. It was not windproof but it was rainproof.

Covered patios today must meet fire codes since the older patios burned in a flash. This means structural posts and beams and coverings similar to the main house. The patio covers come under the structural engineers' specifications. Prior to 1965, a major fire would burn the patio and shortly engulf the entire house. Dangerous fires have a way of changing code requirements.

On your patio, open or closed, you can put an outdoor kitchen with a BBQ, sink, refrigerator, pizza oven (if you do, invite this author to come), fireplace, and fire pit, with seating and a table to enjoy your accomplishments. If your space is larger, add a sofa and chairs. This is a good place to go for tranquility.

It is best to have only movable furniture in order to get as close to the fire pit and table as you see fit. Put seating 15" from your table. Put fire pits 24" or more between seating.

The patio, if not completely covered, can be covered with spaced lattice. If properly set, it will be helpful for using this area at certain times of the day as the sun enters. Space the lattice perpendicular to the sun, the closer the slats, the less of a zebra look.

All of these amenities can be out in the open on the patio without covering, but it does not add a lot to your resale value, although it adds to your personal enjoyment.

It's a Beautiful Day to Be Outdoors

A sun room in a patio that faces south only. The sun will shine in most of the day. The sun room is a good place to put sun-loving plants that you don't want out in the winter or exposed to the elements. The ceiling could be partially glass to let in the sun. This room can be integrated into the main structure, which would add market value.

A sun room, detached from the main house, is called a pergola. A pergola, with its open ceiling structure, can face in any direction. After 4 p.m., the trellis will provide shade.

Of course, you can always mix and match the sun room and the items on your patio. Whatever you do will add appeal to your house. A structural patio cover, more, and open sun rooms, less, but still they will be appealing to the home buyer or appraiser. Have a glass of wine and a toast as you share it with your guest and family.

In Roman times, the patio was a roofless courtyard. Today, the roofless patio is either in the rear or on the side between your house and the property line. You may choose to have two patios: one open and one covered.

The patio is to have a hard surface, such as concrete or paver stones. Lighting is a must. Be prepared for insects in the summertime. There is an array of insect repellant items available today at the home center, hardware store, or even the supermarket.

As mentioned in another segment of this book, the two best deterrents to pests are a living pond with mosquito fish or wild bird feeders to keep the birds feasting on the flying moths and other insects. Caution: the feeders could create weeds so you might want to use a remedy for that—but be sure it is safe for your pets!

Light fixtures can be attached to the house or you can use a lantern light which also adds beauty to your yard. Keep the patio simple, but be sure to add one or more potted plants to create an exemplary example of good design for your guests.

Patio Covers

Patio covers became the rage postwar. For the first time in history, one could sit outside and watch the rain come down while staying dry. The corrugated covering did not last past 1970—for two good reasons. First, the winds would loosen the panels and cause havoc. And two, the big item was that the departments did not approve of this covering for many years without a permit. Perhaps if a permit was issued, they would not blow off. Who knows?

A covered patio, unfortunately, does not add a great deal to the home's resale value. This is one time this author says to put resale aside and put in a covered patio. The structure is to be the same as the house, with the same roofing, but with open walls. Add to the plans and get approval. Improve your lifestyle while living better.

Going beyond the patio is the deck. Do not confuse the platform outside your house at ground level as a deck. A deck is above ground with steps. Period. If you have a downslope lot, then a deck is in order. It can be covered in part or completely.

There is a particular deck that has been incorporated into homes since 1910. That is the second-story deck placed on the second floor over the lower part of the house. This deck, as you can surmise, must be sealed well against water intrusion and has two very big downsides:

First, if you sit out on this deck and look at your neighbor's homes, then think of the neighbors also looking directly into your deck. The author's daughter built such a deck and used it one time. That was it. The good news is that there is always time to enjoy it after sundown!

Second, and the biggest case against a second story deck is obstruction of your view of the yard below. You cannot see what's happening there and that is especially important if you have children. No children? Then think about the resale value. Potential buyers may have children.

Covered Backyard Structures

1. Veranda: A walkway between two structures or leading to a specific part of the yard.
2. Patio: Connected to the house.

3. Pergola: Connected or freestanding but with an open trellis. This is a shady garden structure where there may be vines growing on the sides and roof.

4. Lanai: Fancy name for a roofed patio.

5. Gazebo: A belvedere providing shady space. This small structure is perfect for a wedding (but remember to invite the author).

6. Deck: Usually on the second story and accessed from a bedroom. It can be covered for utilitarian purposes but most are not. A deck is a good place to install an intimate fireplace and sit with friends sipping good wine while gazing at the view.

7. Juliet balcony: There's no room for furniture here as it is only one step out to the railing.

Non-Covered Structures

If you put decking at ground level, it is not a deck no matter what materials you use. Rather, it's considered a landscape finish or part of your landscape—unless, of course, there are stairs leaving to the yard. If the deck is three feet or more off the ground, then a railing must be installed per safety code. You can enclose the deck with wrought iron to give it a personal feeling.

The real structural deck is the cantilever deck, first introduced by architects Buff, Straub and Hensman in the mid 1950s. This deck reaches over the downslope and over the hill. It gives a home without a backyard an outdoor space.

A lot goes into the design of these decks. They must be structurally engineered to be sure it will not move with settling and earthquakes. The wrought iron or glass railing must be 42" in height. Generally, there are no stairs. There are an array of materials to use. In the 1960s, Douglas fir or redwood was used. Today, you only want to use composite material, such as Trex. Research.

Trex was invented by Mobile Oil then the division was sold in 1985. Today, Trex is one of many composite manufacturers that you can choose from. The big factor here is that this material will not show wear during the lifetime of your house. It has the appearance of wood but does not need painting and comes in many colors.

Homeowners say they live on the deck, since it is enclosed and gives a sense of security. This is a fact since there is no way to climb onto the deck from below. Living better!

There are two types of balconies. A balcony is a small deck on the second story, generally no larger than will accommodate a table with two chairs and a lounge chair. Be sure it does not obstruct your view below. The second is a Juliet balcony, mentioned above, which protrudes less than two feet from the wall. You can step out but there is only a small standing space. This is what was profiled in Romeo and Juliet. The patio or deck is living the middle class dream in America.

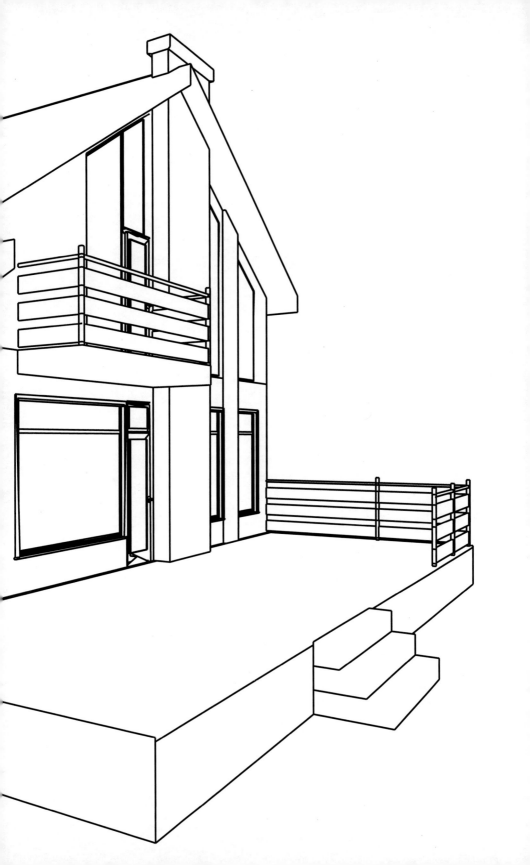

3

Specific Areas

Specific Areas

ELEVATORS AND MORE

Unlock and Unwind

Elevators add a great deal of value to your house. Ask any Realtor. The homes with elevators generally sell for more than asking price. This means, if two homes are identical in size and price, the one with the elevator will sell first and for much more money.

This author's research finds that an elevator defines the house no matter where it is located. Only 2% of homes have elevators in this country. The reason is that following the war, the Baby Boomers were young and felt elevators were not necessary since stairs were easier and quicker. They did not give a second thought to an elevator. But the country is getting older and with a two-story house, the parents are now moving in and some are not able to climb stairs as easily.

If you have a three-story house with the bedrooms on the second floor and recreation/basement below, an elevator is a consideration. In the near future, every three-story house will be equipped with an elevator. This author is further puzzled by why the four-story house in all major cities is not retrofitted with elevators. It takes only the space of a small walk-in closet to install an elevator. The size, of course, depends upon the budget available.

This author suggests looking at a two-person elevator to start. This is easier to fit into the floor plan.

Believe it or not, the cost of an elevator is not prohibitive. If you need to tear up a section of your house to fit an elevator, do it. But for new construction or if it can be constructed easily in an existing building, then do it.

The stair lift is a great feature for an older person. But compare a stair lift, which is not attractive to your staircase, to an elevator designed by your own architect.

Affordable Luxury

There are three elements to consider when designing and installing an elevator: Location, size, and cost. The location must be in the center of the house with the first opening at or near the entry. The opening on the second floor should be in a hallway at the foyer. The basement, or lower level opening, could be anywhere along a wall into a larger room. There's no need for a hallway here.

The author has found it better to have doors on both sides, front and back. On one floor, it opens on one side, and on the other floor, it opens to the opposite side. Consider and plan it. Contact manufacturers and visit some sites. You will learn much.

Let's say you have a two-story house with an elevator. For a little more money, make it go to the roof. At the roof level, build a balcony and enjoy the view, since most likely you will be above all the other homes, or if you have an orchard, there is no better vista.

While there, put in a small fireplace and a small bar which you can stock with your favorite wine. If you do this, invite the author and he will sign this book, and we'll talk about your construction adventure. Share the love!

STAIRCASES

Limited Only by the Imagination

This chapter only addresses the interior staircase. Homes were one-story from the time of Babylon. Multiple stories were constructed only for the hierarchy. For centuries, the middle class did not consider a two-story house since there was generally enough land to build what was required for a one-story house.

With urban development came smaller lots. England was the first in the 3rd century, then France in the 4th century. Smaller lots became a challenge to the builders. They met it head-on with a two-story house—thus, the need for stairs.

The homes were built with family common areas on the first floor and sleeping rooms on the upper level (it was not until the late 1500s that England called the sleeping room a bedroom). This author, after extensive study, summarized that it was called a bedroom because it had a bed in it!

The key factor here is that the staircase was situated at the back of the living room. When going upstairs, a long hall led to the bedrooms, and with larger homes, there would be bedrooms on both sides of the hall. So the middle class second-story home in Europe was a prototype of the houses that we live in today.

Today, 85% of houses are two story, but in the 15th and 16th centuries, only 3% of houses were so built. When Americans first built homes, they were nearly 100% one story. That changed in the 18th century in New York and Philadelphia, two cities with the highest populations.

Why is it that following a major war, new types of buildings were a boom? Following the Civil War, with nothing better to do, the municipalities agreed to divide property into smaller lots. This led to the necessity, as in 15th-century Europe, to build two-story structures. Americans, for the most part, located the staircase at the rear of the living room or near the front door.

The Babylonians first used a ladder, not a staircase, but the upscale steps were made of stone and put in place, usually as wide as six feet. The Romans followed with a tread of about one foot and a rise of about nine inches. The builders thought these steps, since made of stone, would last forever.

Today, two millennium later, they were correct. Most stone stairs are in their original order except for one thing: they are worn. The stone used was relatively soft and the stairs found in Europe are worn down by about 40%, but many stone stairs outlasted their houses.

Center Focus

Wood stairs were first used in England about the year 400. Not until then were many houses built with two stories. In this country, wood staircases were built as early as the 16th century. The wood, of course, was Douglas fir. Fir stairs looked great, didn't have much grain, and were easy to fabricate. But fir only lasts forty years or so before showing substantial wear. Today, fir wood is only used for the second staircase, such as stairs to the basement.

Oak stairs are much more durable and were introduced in the 19th century. About the time of the Civil War, oak trees were not plentiful on the East Coast because the wood was difficult to come by. Then along came the logging companies. They not only cut down the oaks, they planted five oaks for every one cut. The average oak tree grows for five years before it is cut down and used for your staircase. You may feel the oaks should not be cut down, but these are not your yard trees. They are in a forest not visible by the general public.

The area of oaks in 1775 was about 1,900 square miles. The area of oak trees in this country today, primarily in North Carolina, is about 2.6 million. This means that the oak will increase in maturity faster than it will be cut down in our lifetime. Once the oak industry took hold around 1945, oak was requested by all architects.

Oak was also first used for cabinets around 1970. It was the number one choice of hardwood floors until 2001 when composite came on the market. From 1850 until 1905, cabinets were made primarily from fir since Douglas fir was plentiful due to its fast growth.

In the 1960s, the country saw every home change to natural wood. No, not oaks, but ash and birch. During the 1960s and 1970s, all natural wood cabinets were built with either ash or birch wood. Okay, so why aren't there ash or birch staircases?

This author thinks the ash and birch trend lasted for such a short time that it could not infiltrate. Oak became *king* because of its durability and remains so today.

Outstanding Decisions

In many parts of this country, oak trees are protected from removal. Rightfully so, they are a beautiful, if not the most beautiful, tree—especially the live oak. Curve the stairs if you can afford them. If you actually can afford to do that, then this author could use a loan!

If you have the space for single or double curved stairs, then make them as nice as you can. What are nice are oak treads and oak risers with oak railings.

Upgrade? Use marble treads and risers and wrought iron railings. Railing heights are a newer code requirement. Don't be caught with a railing costing as much as this author's first house that does not meet code. A simple phone call to the permit department is all that's required to find answers. Make sure you get that person's name and position. Ask about the railing height requirements. Incorrect railing height means the railing cannot be altered; it must be rebuilt.

All this can change in an instant. First you plan the stairs at one location, then you discover, after you lay out your second floor, that the stair location won't work. Simple! Relocate the stairs. Stairs do not dictate your second-floor plan. Your second-floor plan dictates the location of the stairs. It's called flexibility! As a matter of fact, everything you do is subject to flexibility. If you must have a straight staircase, put it in.

Safety Can Save Lives

Now the planning. When planning for a two-story house, begin with the placement of the front door. Always. It has to be in the center or near the center of the front of your house. Then design the staircase. This is to be done before any other rooms are positioned on either level.

Draw in the staircase of your choice: curved, straight, or turned part way. This author strongly recommends against a straight staircase. Sometimes if cannot be avoided but a straight staircase is dangerous for children and the elderly. If you have no other choice than to design a straight staircase, then put in motion lights, top and bottom. In fact, put in motion lights where you think it is proper

Before motion lights were invented, so many elderly, losing their sense of location, stepped into the darkened staircase and met their maker. Turned stairs also help the elderly catch their breath, and at the same time, slow down the children. This author feels it's more enjoyable to go upstairs with a landing. Less huffing and puffing.

Your staircase requirements may be as simple as wood painted steps and railing or as elaborate as a wrought iron railing, double curved. No matter what, they all have something in common: the first step must be visible from the front door.

Okay, you surmised, with prodding from this author, that the staircase is to be part of the entry. The staircase in the entry is called a "prime location." If it is located elsewhere, in the hall or family room and not visible from the front door, it is in a secondary location.

Let's say you put the staircase in back of your house, not visible from the entry, and someone enters your foyer and says to you, "I thought you had a two-story house?" You answer, "We do." They then ask, "Then where are the stairs?"

Never let this happen. Avoid it at all costs. If an acquaintance questions this poor staircase location, then you can bet the resale of your house will drop significantly.

Some homeowners and guests, just out of bed, do not want to come down the stairs in order to go to the other parts of the house. If this is a concern, put in a secondary staircase directly or near the kitchen or lower hallway.

Your house is not that large that your lifestyle of coming down the stairs into the entry may have to be adjusted. This is based on the fact that there are no persons milling around in your entry or in the closets, so let's say it's relatively safe.

In short, your staircase should be a showcase. Make it as nice as your budget warrants. Consider an oak step with a wood railing.

Paint the risers white, paint the balusters and side skirts white with oak treads and oak handrails. It will be a showcase staircase.

To verify:

- Stair treads are what you step on.
- Risers are at the back of the stairs.
- The landing is what you step onto after opening the door.
- Balusters are the uprights between the steps and the railing.

As for the area under the stairs, you can leave that space open or enclose it for use as a powder room (although it's better to have the powder room off the hallway), coat closet, or coat and shoe closet. Or, if you have an extra kid, then he can live there.

FLOOR COVERING

Attention to Details

When it comes to department inspections, all that is needed is one coat of paint on the floors. That paint on the floors is for sanitation purposes.

How many centuries have gone by with a dirt floor? The reason for this is simple: There was nothing available to cover these floors except wooden planks. The planks were laid on the floor tightly with joints filled with soil to prevent creatures from coming through. The wood used was forested in the area.

In this country, cedar and pine was primarily used. But after a half century, the wood became termite-infested. The homeowners from the 16th century and for 200 years after that time, used cedar, ash, or birch wood. All became infested. It was not until the 18th century that it was discovered that redwood would resist termites. But redwood was hard to come by since a majority of the trees were grown in the western part of the United States.

Then along came the revolution of flooring. Floors were built at least one foot above the ground, since subterranean termites come from the soil beneath. The one-foot construction started in the 18th century and lasted until about 1920.

The down side, and it was a big one, was that there was little or no crawl space under the house to do any plumbing repairs. If there was a leak in the drain lines, it could not be fixed from the underside. If there was a sewer leak under the floor, which was underground, there would not be a detection. If there was a clog, that would have entailed a major repair. Sewer lines were installed under the house, for as long as cities have had street sewers.

In 1930 a big correction came about. Nearly all departments required an 18" crawl space under the house, which is the rule today. This is not only termite-resistant, but enables workmen to crawl under the house to repair and install new lines. Since then, the term "crawl space" has come about, as well as the term "raised foundation," most commonly known as "conventional floor construction."

Walk on a Cloud

Then along came concrete slab floors. There are fewer, if any, houses built today on grade that are not on a concrete slab floor. There is a huge advantage to having concrete floors. The biggest reason is cost. If developers build with concrete floors, why not you? Whether you are building new or adding on, use concrete floors, also known as "slab floors."

You may think that slab floors make it impossible to access drain and sewer lines, but with the innovation of ABS, there is no need for access since the lines will be intact for more than a century. That is as long as you will live in it. Also, the new copper lines put under the slab will stay intact without trouble since there are no connections to leak. Today, copper is laid in one piece underground. Use only type "L" for thicker copper walls.

Another big factor to consider is termite resistance. There is always a possibility of subterranean termites coming through a crack, but they are not structurally detrimental. Not a factor—no worries.

Every structural engineer ties the slab to the foundation with what is called "rebar" (steel rods generally ½" in diameter). This makes your house safer during earthquakes and hurricanes. The building departments are favorable to slab construction. It is not required, but recommended.

How many homes have you been in that slope due to settling, or have hardwood floors that squeak or bounce when you walk on them? None of these will happen with slab floors. Point taken!

Composite Floor Coverings

Hardwood floors are still used in 80% of all homes today. But in about twenty-five years, that number will decrease to less than 20%. The reason is the innovation of composite flooring. Most composite flooring is scratch resistant. More and more homeowners have dogs that stay primarily in the house and dogs have a tendency to scratch flooring. This is a big selling point.

Up until the 20th century, dogs were left outside. Dogs then were primarily used to protect against intruders, such as animals and sometimes, bill collectors. Today, in America, dogs stay in more than 75% of homes. All the more reason to have scratch-resistant flooring.

Scratch-resistant flooring, also known as composite, can be laid on both raised wood and slab floors. Some brands make it look so close to wood that you can hardly tell the difference. An added feature is most can be used on kitchen and bath floors because they are water–resistant. Want wood floors everywhere? Now, tile is like wood—but better. Great!

Another option is tile. There are tiles that are patterned to look like wood. But the hardwood look may not be what you want for some areas. The entry should look separate from the main part of the house. The entry should be congruent. Tile the entry and if you have enough space, put in a floor medallion. A medallion below your entry chandelier will make your entry elegant.

This author bought a medallion but did not realize the labor that was required to fit the tile around it. You should budget accordingly. A medallion, either round or square, is a computer-designed pattern often imprinted in granite or marble.

Tile the kitchen and bath floors with composite and continue the flooring into the kitchen, as many are doing today. Composite will hold up just fine in the kitchen and with give the kitchen an open look. This is the way to go.

If you have a delineation between your kitchen and family room, you can choose tile. Delineation, in this sense, means no cabinets or stools are partly on the dividing line. This does not have to match the entry. The entry tile and tile work is perhaps more than you want in the kitchen: marble in the entry and porcelain or travertine in the kitchen.

The master bath floor must be tiled. Make sure the installer sets the tile at the same level as the adjacent hardwood floors. This can be achieved using the proper mastic and underlayment. You can choose the tile to be laid straight or diagonally. Use 12" x 12" tile for the floor, no matter what other sizes are available—unless you put in accents. Your designer knows!

Where Beauty Sets In

Also available is a heat-treated tile floor. This is a method where, by running wires under the tile, it heats up the floor. The down side is that you have to switch on the elements in advance. The bigger down side is, if a portion goes out, you have no way to fix it. So put in a heated floor and take your chances. It may not be worth the investment. You may not want a heated floor during really warm weather, but….

You may have a contemporary house so the tile exterior flows into the interior using the same material. The family room and patio need to have the same tile, bringing the outside in. When you are walking on your floors, your eye will not lead you to the walls or other part of your house—it will lead you to your flooring. Will you love your decision? Yes!

Then the exterior may have to be 1" lower than the interior, per department requirement, unless you devised a system for the water to flow away from the house at 2%. This can more easily be achieved if you have a patio covering.

If you are not sold on hardwood and tile due to the cold floors, consider carpet. In the 1950s, shag carpet was the rage, but the preferred carpet today is a close knit. You can put this in any room but the choice today are only the bedrooms. Old vacuum for sale. It's just collecting dust.

It's unfortunate that homeowners today must endure the coldness of hardwood and tile floors with bare feet. Think of it as you would in having to stop at a sign even though no other cars are near—roll with the punches. Use socks! This author may be a weirdo (per wife) but walking on a cooler floor is therapy—go figure! Use socks or wear slippers.

You may want to get the advice of an interior designer but don't be swayed. You decide what materials you want to use and where. Leave it to the designer to come up with the product, colors, and layout. Best of both worlds! Elixir!

DOORS

Spruce Up Your House

Doors are an integral part of your house. They are used for privacy, sound deadening, and to ingress and egress. Get ready for this one: All exterior residential doors must swing in. All commercial doors must swing out. If you are leaving any commercial building built in the last century, the entry/exit door swings out. The reason is for fire safety.

In the event of a commotion of any kind going on inside, a speedy exit is necessary. Don't hesitate. Push the door since it will swing out. This is a code requirement. No commercial door today is wood since wood weathers when swinging out. They are made primarily of aluminum or other weather-proof metals. These doors, if properly hinged and maintained, will last the duration of the building.

Residential doors are just the opposite. The door swings in. Have you ever seen a home's front door swing out? The entry door has been around from the time of Babylon when all front doors swung in.

This holds true for side and rear doors too. It's a misconception that swing-in doors take up more room. Not close to being true. If you stand in front of an exterior door, you take up nine square feet of space. If the door swings in or out, it still takes up nine square feet of space. You gain no space by swinging out.

Also close an out-swinging door in the rain, get wet! This author wonders why architects still swing doors out. If they, themselves, had an out-swinging door that deteriorated, they would go back to the drawing board. Wood doors that swing out have a lifespan of ten years. Be proactive.

Also, a closed but swinging door has visible hinges. If a door opens out, then you see hinges. No big deal until the unthinkable happens. A burglar who sees a door with hinges can simply pop up the hinge pins and pry the door open. The door lock is not effective. Gone are your Elvis Presley discs. Use stainless steel screen wire for safety.

Okay, so you forgot your house key. Now you know how to break into your house. If the door swings in, call a locksmith.

Improve Your Lifestyle

Weather stripping and door shoes came on the scene around 1955 but did not get fully implemented until a decade later. The building departments did not require this insulation until 1970. Now, you must install weather stripping (a vinyl or rubber insulation set into the jamb) and a door shoe of aluminum and vinyl at the bottom of the door. This keeps out the elements and the pests.

Poor insects, they no longer can get in!

Additionally, a large overhang above your door is advisable along with an awning. Cloth awnings hold up for 15 years or more. Aluminum is better, but less attractive.

Bottom line: If you insist on doors opening out, you should not be reading this book. This book is to tell you—not to suggest to you. And if you don't agree, then why not sell your house for less? Drastic comment but it has merit.

Locks

Some rooms require interior door locks. There are three kinds of locks:

1. Passage—a door from room to room without a lock.

2. Privacy—does not have a key lock.

3. Key—for an exterior or an interior door.

Privacy locks are either knob or handle opening. Use these on bathroom and the master bedroom doors. You can put privacy locks on other bedrooms and install them as you see fit. A good example: Your in-laws visit frequently and wander throughout the house so this might necessitate a privacy lock. When the children get older, change the locks from passage to privacy. It's a simple job for Mr. Handyman.

Okay, so you have a nice house but you want more security in the master bedroom. Put in surface bolts. These are flat bolts which will secure your room beyond the door lock.

Has a Good Ring to It

In the past, doors varied in size, but today they are becoming more standard. The entry door in 95% of homes is 36 " wide. Interior doors are best at 30" wide, which will accommodate a wheelchair. During the end of the last century, many departments required 32" room doors (some still do). Their requirement was to accommodate the handicapped. Now it has been determined that the handicapped can maneuver through a 30" opening.

A barn door for the bath is a good choice because the door swinging in is difficult for wheelchairs.

A walk-up door can be as small as 18" to 24" wide. These are not walk-through doors but rather, are used only to open and get items on a shelf, such as you would need for linen, the kitchen pantry or a closet.

There are two places to put a double door. Use double-door entry doors if you have the room. The trend today is away from double doors to a single door with two side lights (12" – 18")and fixed window panels to match the front door. Most developers are sticking to the one 36" door. This is a good place to consider leaded glass in the door and side lights.

Digital locks are easy to use. Punch in the numbers—easy when loaded down with groceries. Set the lock to close automatically after each use.

The other place for double doors is the master bedroom. Whomever sees these doors knows instinctively that it leads to the master bedroom. Only if you have the space though. They do not have to be equal in size—as long as one is 30" wide.

Sliding glass exterior doors have been around since 1952. If you see a house with sliding doors (called patio doors), you know the house was built after 1952. You now have the choice of a single slider or a double slider with fixed panels at one or both ends. Common size is a 12-foot unit. Each panel is four feet wide. There are unending options. These doors also have exterior screens. Doors now come with breakthrough shatter-proof glass, similar to car windows.

The future house (almost here) will have sliders that collect to one side. This will open the family room wall and open to insects. There are certain times of the year when insects are not a problem. Time to open the wall and have a party. Remember to invite the author.

The barn door is the rage. This author believes this phenomenon will last for a short twenty years and go out like the white appliances did. Hotels all over the globe are putting barn doors between the bath and toilet compartments. The kids love barn doors and want them between their bedroom and their private bath. Put barn doors wherever you can. Beside the kid's bath, pantry, linen closets, and closets. What is behind the door? Only you will know.

WINDOWS

A Clear View

This author takes note that the igloo and the tepee had no windows but still functioned as a house. These houses function quite well without windows. The only openings were the doorway and the vented opening. Modern times calls for windows for both view and ventilation. The question is: how much view and how much ventilation?

From Ancient China to post World War I, women wanted the windows for light and ventilation. The men were out doing their thing but the women were in the house most of the time.

There are minimum requirements for windows, but no maximum. There are two obvious reasons for windows: light and ventilation. Many municipalities require a minimum of 8% of the floor space to be glass, and half, or 4%, of that to be operable. These requirements were changed from a ratio of 10/5 around 2015. The reason for less glass requirements was for energy conservation.

The energy aspect of windows has not caught up to technology. The energy engineers calculated the heat loss of single-pane glass. Today, double-pane windows are most common. There are also triple-pane glass and commercial-insulated glass, which is used in some residential homes.

Prior to the turn of the 20th century, all windows were wood with strips of wood to seal them. Then the evolution began. First, during the early 20th century, steel windows were manufactured and made for every home. The windows had putty to insulate the edges of the glass. This was done professionally by a glazer in the shop and sometimes on the site. The problem was that they did not hold the test of time. After about 25 years, the putty began to crack and fall out. One reason was that the average homeowner did not paint every five years as the manufacturer suggested.

The first wood windows were double hung. This means both the top and bottom slide. The top slides down and the bottom goes up. When closed, they had a turned latch. Unfortunately, a burglar easily broke the glass to get at the latch to open and crawl in. Today, the glass is double pane and mostly tempered and the latches are difficult to maneuver from the outside.

Sliders

Windows now come with either of two functions: they slide up and down or side to side. Most homes have side sliders since they are easier to operate. Caution, do not use tall but narrower windows since they will become more difficult to slide and lock. Plan on the operational section to be no more than two times the height compared to the width. Research.

Sliders are the easiest kind of window for children to operate. A majority of windows are half operable and half fixed. The terms XO and OX are used in the industry. Standing facing the window from inside your room, the part of the window which moves is the X and the portion fixed is the O. If you have a window where the right side moves and the left side is fixed, then you have an XOX.

These three-section windows are primarily used above beds or for very large windows, but the manufacturer limits the size of glass frames they produce. Use only stainless steel screens. Research.

This leads to the maximum size glass as seen in ever-increasing contemporary homes. Entire walls of glass. The glass wall facing the northern view is ideal to reduce sunlight and heat intrusion.

No matter what style home you desire, your plans must pass through an energy engineer's calculation for heat loss. Energy engineering is the fastest growing profession in this building industry. Departments, homeowners, and developers rely on their calculations to better open the walls to views without the loss of energy.

Contemporary is for the select few. So come back to earth and discuss your windows. To begin, single-pane windows are no longer available in this country. Double pane is only available, and that is what you want, period!

You'll Love What You See

There is another window configuration to consider. Casement windows are windows that open completely out by way of an inside crank. The screen is on the inside. On a one-story house, this window may damage the head of the gardener working close to the house, or you, if you are outside the window. They may be a good option on the second story.

Be cautious of casement windows, which can be difficult to latch. Smaller casements will generally work fine, but larger casements may not hold up in time. Research.

Fixed windows can be used anywhere ventilation is not required. Put a fixed window at the top of the stairs, garage, side of front door, or bath, as long as the room has a ventilation fan. A ventilation fan is a good investment.

No matter how much glass is required, do what you want to do. Keep in mind that lots of glass means little wall space. When was the last time you saw a picture hanging on a glass wall? Furniture in front of the glass is okay as long as it looks good from the outside. You have heard the term "living in a glass house"? Okay, not the same.

By 2020, only 5% of the homes built will be of glass walls. One other reason for this low percentile is the huge cost of construction. Glass walls, as compared to standard construction, are double to five-times the cost. With that said, by 2050, about 15% of homes will have glass walls, but the view inside will be clear looking out, while the view looking from the outside will be dark. New innovations. Stick around!

Aluminum windows were invented by the International Window Company of Los Angeles. They still make aluminum frames, but vinyl is preferred. Vinyl windows hold up better than any other frames on the market, and therefore, are used in 95% of all new and replacements.

Steel windows were not sliders; they were casements. The screen was on the inside, a crank was used to operate. An additional problem was if the house settled, as they did back then, due to inadequate foundations, they would not close tight. Since insulation around the panels was not implemented yet, they would not close tight and bugs came in. The screen was a deterrent, but not foolproof.

Steel window manufacturers did not last long—about seventy-five years max. Today, there are a few steel-framed companies, but in 1945, there were more than 100. Aluminum units were available in all sizes. They were inexpensive compared to wood and had better longevity. But there was a downside. Even though aluminum had baked-on finishes, the joints showed of rust. Not good. Not accepted. Due to the makeup of the frames and sash, the window had no character. It did not have curb appeal. Windows were single pane, which did not insulate well and were not tamper proof.

Around 1980, everything changed. Vinyl windows, although first introduced in 1940, became the window of demand. But with vinyl windows came another revolution—double-pane glass.

Lots of Windows

Energy-efficient, double-pane glass works so well that building departments across the country demanded that it be used everywhere. When it comes to regulation, this author takes issue with so many regulations, but with double-pane glass, no issue. The "R" value (or efficiency value. "R" is the value given to heat escaping the house) of a window's single-pane glass is three, but with double-pane glass, it is ten. It has more than three times the insulation. This does not allow much heat to enter. It keeps your heated room warmer.

First introduced in the mid-century, vinyl had a fading factor. Not good. It took a few more years with laboratory testing to find a formula for vinyl that would not fade or yellow. Once this was accomplished, the popularity took off.

Vinyl windows replaced wood, steel, and aluminum. Today, vinyl is requested by nearly all developers, so why not you? Remember that the developer does everything for resale value. Some want the wood look of old. The vinyl window with its thick sash frame resembles wood. It does not replace wood, but it comes close. Plus vinyl comes in many colors. Most are white. Never needs painting.

The most popular aluminum color is dark bronze. Bronze tone is not available in vinyl, mostly pastel. Doors are made of aluminum and with a bronze tone. The bronze tone will not show rust. The down side is most homeowners prefer white. White: today, tomorrow, and beyond. Guaranteed. But with contemporary homes which do not live in the realm of ordinary, the bronze aluminum metal is used extensively. Most commercial frames on doors and windows are bronze-tone aluminum as well as natural.

If you are of the small 5% of people who desire a contemporary home style, you may want to visit Ascaya in Henderson, Nevada. Once there, you will not want to leave—if you can afford it. Contemporary architecture has evolved from the architecture of Frank Lloyd Wright in 1940 to Ascaya. As the good contractor said, "We do windows."

Window Grids

Grids are used to divide a pane of window glass into smaller sections, usually about one square foot. The term "mullions" was used until 1950 until "grids" became the term used by manufacturers.

Window grids were first introduced in England in the 13th century and adopted all over Europe in the 15th century. They were first introduced in America in the 17th century, but took hold in the 18th century. Grids took a while to be incorporated in the American home. Wood windows had grids in the front only until the 20th century.

Wood window grids were true divided panes about one inch in thickness and were puttied. Then along came the wood grids without putty. These windows became the rage from 1700 to 1955 when aluminum windows came on the market with grids glued to the windows without *true divided*.

Today, vinyl windows come in the true divided (each section of glass separated by a mullion). But along came the biggest innovation in grid windows, largely manufactured by Milgard Window

Company. The grids were put between two sections of double pane glass. This is widespread today in all developments and the average American home.

Having grids between the glass makes for the best possible insulation, looks good (some sculptured grids have the appearance of wood), and best of all, allows the windows to be easily cleaned.

Windows with grids between two sheets of glass meets code requirements and are energy-efficient. Now the misconception: homeowners like the grid look so they put it on all windows, everywhere. Wrong! Grids should only be in the front of the house for aesthetic purposes and not at the rear of the house. The rear windows should be clear of grids for a clear view of the backyard and beyond.

Grids in the front of most traditional homes and no grids at the rear. Period! Grids are available in patio doors, but don't request it. Grids obstruct view.

Also available today are leaded glass windows. Prior to 1975, leaded glass windows did not pass energy requirements. The simple answer is to put the leaded glass configuration in a double-pane frame. Therefore, the double pane meets requirements and added is the leaded or stained glass you want. This is good for front-door side lights, baths, and top of stairs. Costly, yes, but appealing.

With that said, homes are becoming less grid oriented but you are remodeling now to blend in with the neighborhood, so what do you care about the desires thirty years from now? All you want to do is to improve your lifestyle.

ROOFING

Put the Edge in Educate

For decades, roofs were made with a straw called thatch (so these roofs were appropriately called thatched roofs). Straw could be tightly bundled to keep out a majority of rain water. In many parts of Europe, palm fronds were traded for a better roof covering, their super-fibrous leaves lasting many years before deteriorating. They are so durable that they can not be composted. They are too fibrous.

When wood roofs were introduced in 13th century Europe, they needed a better covering. Along came clay roofs. Clay was spread over the wood and roof and did its job. Unfortunately, the clay contracted and left gaps which had to be filled by the roofing company or the homeowner.

Thus originated the first outside contractor or, in a later case, subcontractor.

About this time, an entrepreneur with ingenuity came up with clay tiles. Clay tiles, in various shapes and forms, were the option of all builders from 1500 to the present day in Europe and elsewhere. America did not grasp this concept until 1750. This author is puzzled as to why it took so long for this country to use clay tiles. In 1835, the first cement tile was used in America. Clay tile would definitely last fifty years, but cement tile roofs in Europe have lasted 200 or more years.

Cement tiles come in only two shapes: *flat tile*, laid in even rows with a hook at the top to keep it in line and hold them in place, and the popular *tops and pans* which has been the number one choice in Europe.

A picturesque drive from Paris, France to the French Riviera takes about two days. Along this drive, you will see nothing but tops and pans roofs. If you go anywhere in Europe, you will find tops and pans. This means the one tile is laid up and the next tile is laid over the edges, leaving good drainage. The down side of tops and pans is that there are spaces for pests to sneak in.

One solution to minimize the problem is to use "S" tile. "S" tile has fewer gaps. The objective is to seal all possible openings. It will come close but not 100%.

This is a trade-off for sure: rodents getting in versus longevity. Be aware, the steeper the roof, the longer it will last. That is why steep thirty-year roofs called composition have lasted seventy-five years. When it comes to concrete tile roofs, steepness doesn't matter as much.

Keeps You Covered

Let us not continue without mentioning other roof types that may fit your project. Composite roofing has evolved from a nail-down to a torch-down application. This is good for a flat or nearly flat roof. Also, for this flat roof, gravel or rock is in order. The roofer applies hot tar with a mop which is pumped from a kettle near the street. Then rock is spread over the hot tar. It's an old fashioned method with current-day results.

Today, there are thirty-year, forty-year, and fifty-year roofing materials. A 30-year roof should last thirty years before needing to be replaced. A forty-year roof should last forty years, and a fifty-year roof should last a lifetime.

A thirty-year roof is what the industry called *3-tab shingles*. A century ago, 90% of all roofs in this country were 3-tab as they were easy to install by the average craftsman since the shingles came in bundles and fit one against the other with an overlap to make it waterproof. The shingles were upgraded in 1950 to have a tar tab, which, when the sun heated them, welded them into each other. This was not only waterproof, it was wind resistant.

Wife to husband: "The roof is leaking." No wonder—it's raining.

In the 1950s, the builder gave no other thought to any other roofing materials. Homes one century later still had the thirty-year, 3-tab shingles, but over the last seventy years, a forty-year roof replaced the thirty-year, 3-tab. On existing homes, it became the desired roofing for new construction. The forty-year roof became known as dimensional. Cost over 30-year, about 40% more. Cost of cement-tile roofing, about 50% more.

The metal roof, also known as "steel roof," is an option if your house is modern or a current style. This roofing has improved since being introduced in 1960. This roof is quieter but not quiet—you will hear the rain. This type of roofing is used extensively on commercial properties for its durability. The cost is much more though. Only a few roofers are capable of doing this task. If you desire a metal roof, then most likely, you will hire a commercial roofer to do the job. The cards are out on metal roofing. Only time will tell.

If you care to look to the future, then the roofing will be solar tiles. Using solar tiles would be ahead of our time. Tesla has introduced solar tiles. Putting these tiles in lieu of conventional shingles is a chance you have to take, as far as their future performance. First weigh their appearance.

This author believes that in the 22nd century, all roofs will have solar capabilities. That is later, much later, but at least you know what your grandchildren will be living under.

Pleasurable Appearance

Let's come back to earth. The roof you choose today should be what is done on your block or in your community—returning back to resale value.

Solar shingles should not be confused with solar panels. Installing solar panels, as aforementioned, does not pencil out at all. Definite! Shingles are more attractive and may cover your electrical costs to run your home. Solar panels will not do the job, period! Also, keep in mind that shingles can be walked upon without damage, as compared to concrete tiles that can crack when walked upon improperly. Do not allow an unknowledgeable person to walk on tile roofs. There is no problem with asphalt or metal roofs. If you have or propose to use concrete tile, then only a trained professional should walk on the roof.

There is an additional downside to concrete tiles. Older homes with tiles were required to have one layer, felt, as protection underneath. After forty years, the felt deteriorated, causing leaks. The roofing then had to be removed, the underlayment replaced, and the tile reset, which was costly. Today, the required underlayment will hold up for many years to come.

This leads us back to solar panels. If your roof needs replacing and you have solar panels, the cost, overall, may put you into the poor house.

GUTTERS

Hit the Nail on the Head

No gutters. You read this right. Do not install gutters unless the upper section (second story) drains on a lower roof. Gutters accumulate leaves over a period of time which will cause water to deteriorate the wood overhang. Any 100-year-old house with gutters has deteriorated wood at the eves causing rot and termites.

If you live in the desert with not much rain, you do not need gutters. If you live in areas with lots of rain, the gutters will overflow. This author saw a lot of water running over nice copper gutters—only 20% of the water goes through the down spout. They are not a good investment.

From postwar to 1968, officials required gutters to keep water from rushing into the streets. Later the requirement was dropped since it became better to allow roof water to percolate into the landscape.

Gutters can also kill. Gutters hold water which is backed up by leaves which you cannot see from the ground level. Mosquitos are attracted, and they could carry the West Nile virus that can lead to death.

If you really want gutters, be sure the gutter is 6" wide and has a large downspout. Better, but not best. Discriminating home buyers don't care about gutters. Really!

Venting the attic requires the following: First, lower or custom vents at the gable ends or on the roof. The roof vents for composition roofs are called dormer vents. They come in various sizes. The architect should calculate (but seldom does) the number of vents required. This is a calculation of the square inch of the vent to the floor space (attic space). The more the vents, the cooler your house will be.

Go into the attic with limited vents on a hot day and the temperature will be twenty to thirty degrees hotter. Not good. Put in the prescribed vents (solar vents are also effective). The solar turbine spins the heat outward.

Ventilating fans at the gable ends are also good. They are on a thermostat which works very well. For tile roofs, there are the flat vents to blend with the roof. All vents should be primed properly and painted to match the color of the roofing tile. This painting process should be redone every ten to fifteen years by a professional who knows how to walk on the tile roofing.

Keep in mind, when choosing roofing, the large majority of your house as viewed from the street can be the roof. It could be as much as 35% of your house. Get the returns you want! Put the edge in educate.

Finials, also called "hip knob," is an element of copper or aluminum, emphasizing a corner of a roof gable. It is also used on the top of domes. You can put one or more on your roof and it will look outstanding.

ELECTRICAL AND LIGHTING

Improving Your Quality of Life

Electricity is relatively new to the civilized world. Or you might say electricity gave cause for the civilized world to become generated!

Electricity in our country is continuously evolving. Safe and more efficient energy is continuously being invented—the television is a perfect example. First came the tubes, then came the tubeless. First came the 10" and, much later, the stadium size.

In the 19th century, every home had "knob and tube" electricity. The objective was to separate the incoming and outgoing links with a spacer. Knob and tube electrical system lasted 85 years until the coated wire was introduced by the Americans in 1936, which also introduced safety standards.

Electrical lines no longer needed to be separated since the separation was inside the cable. There are fewer than 18% of homes still in this country with knob and tube electricity. The present generation may not ever see knob and tube unless they see the demolition of these houses or part of that house.

But there is one underlying factor inherent in this country and that is safety. The safety of electrical installations along with stronger concrete foundations are what makes American homes better. This is made possible because of the engineers' recommendations to the building departments to require safety standards.

Want to live in this country? You will get the absolute best the professionals have to offer while improving the quality of your life.

The average homeowner spends less time making an electrical plan for their home than shopping for appliances, but electrical and lighting could add up to the same overall costs of appliances. These average 15% of the overall construction costs.

At the end of the 19ᵗʰ century, there was one electrical outlet per wall in every major room. Some homes had two. Today, only 120 years later, there is one outlet per wall in major rooms. In the near future, with more and more electrical items being remote, there will be fewer to none at all. But let us state today, we need outlets. First and foremost, there are building requirements. One outlet is required six feet from a door and twelve feet along the wall with four to a major room, minimum. Outlets (also known as wall plugs) are 16" from the floor and 42" from the floor for a desk or workbench.

Living the Fullest

Some architects layout electrical and lighting without taking the time to evaluate what is needed. For today's lifestyle, seldom does the architect make outlet provisions for the tankless water heater, wall televisions, security outlets, and Christmas lighting switches and outlets. Sometimes, architects and designers will put in too many recess fixtures. You, then, have to resort to dimmers to reduce the amount of light, which is not cost effective.

An outlet is required on the side of a washbasin and if there are two basins, two are required. In the kitchen, it's required to have one outlet at each work station, meaning both sides of the sink and both sides of the range, if there is a counter. Becoming more required is one outlet at the side of an island, which is very convenient. Both sides of the island is better.

Adding electrical beyond standard department requirements is up to you. They may not be required or regulated. Be sure you put an outlet for the tankless water heater, television, office equipment, outdoor Christmas lights, and something often overlooked—landscape outlets, a.k.a. junction boxes. There may be a special occasion when something needs to be plugged in outside. Put in many junction boxes. It's better to do it during the electrical stage than after walkways are poured. Put a junction outlet at each area of the rear yard. Only your designer will know!

Consider outlets on both sides of the beds. It may cost extra but the cost is minimal during construction. Adding them later can be expensive. Knocking holes in the wall and digging under walkways are never in the budget.

Staircases must have one or more lights with switches at the top and bottom of the stairs.

Your electrical panel and size should be wisely considered. The panel with circuit breakers is placed on the exterior, but the city or county electrical company will want to spot the panel location to better suit their requirements, such as the closest distance to their power source. The power company has no say when it comes to the size of the panel. Panel is where meter and circuit breakers are located. They are only concerned about two things: overhead or underground wires to your house.

If you have a choice, choose underground. Older over-ground wires can be damaged by the elements and the furry animals and it is difficult to locate a spot of a ruptured wire. Today, it's easier to locate your stolen car in another state than it is to find the damage to an overhead wire. Today, wires are made of steel but if the line comes into your house by way of a tree, then guess who will be walking the tightrope right into your attic?

In the Current

Power poles are becoming a thing of the past. As more and more wind and rain disasters in this country occur, the fewer power poles you will see, and certainly not wood poles. All new land developments have underground wire requirements. Safe? Absolutely! You can tell the age of a newer development by the height of mature trees with no power poles visible.

Your electrical panel must be 200 amperage, minimum. In this country, you cannot find a new panel less than 200 amperage. The reason is that there are so many electrical needs and installations that only a 200-amp panel can supply efficient electricity.

The next upsize is a 400-amperage panel. This author has not been privy to anything larger in a residential, middle-class home. A 400 amp will service up to a 10,000 square-foot house and maybe somewhat larger. But it does not end there.

The main panel feeds a subpanel or subpanels. Many larger homes have as many as six subpanels. A subpanel is used to reduce the many lines from the main panel. Instead, one larger line feeds a subpanel with ten or more breakers. This is good if you need to flip a breaker during inclement weather. You don't have to go outside in the rain to the main panel. You can simply go to the closest subpanel.

A subpanel can be put in the laundry, pantry or hallway. This author has a subpanel in the hallway. There is a picture of James Dean which slides to one side to expose the panel. When the wife walks by, she throws a kiss. Revolting!

The big advantage of having subpanels is that if properly marked, it will give you a chance to trip on the breaker or see which breaker has been tripped. The breaker will show off. You need to trip it to "on" in order for electricity to pass. If it won't trip to "on," then call an electrician to fix the problem.

Remember one big item: be sure the electrician labels each breaker correctly. More often than not, the inspector will require labeling prior to signing off on the final inspection. But they do not check accuracy. That is up to you. Request a meeting with the electrician to show you how it is labeled before the job is complete.

A Reflection of You

Thinking you thought we would get into this section sooner than later. One century ago, all rooms had one ceiling light (called a surface light) and one switch. Everyone was satisfied with that since it lit up the room. What could be better? Well the answer, not much. One light in the center of the ceiling is all we need today.

Let us be more astute. Some rooms can still have one light in the ceiling but other rooms need more. The bedrooms, other than the master, can have one light in the center and no more, but multiple bulbs are good in the one center light with a dimmer. Also consider a fan with a light which looks great year-round for circulating air.

The master bedroom requires a center light with a dimmer. Additionally, recess lights above the bed that are controlled by switches from both sides for reading. Good time to read this book!

Then along came LED: Light Emitting Diode. From 1938 to 2012, most bulbs were incandescent, but now they are primarily LED. Put LED everywhere a recess light is planned. No more fluorescent and no more incandescent lights. It's 100% LED until something better comes along.

LED entered the scene in 2002 but not until 2012 did LED become widespread in this country. There are three illuminated LED recess lights. First, the 27K, a warmer light but not as bright. Then the 40K, very bright and cool. The 30K is most commonly used. It can also be dimmed; (LED dimmers were not available prior to 2000). The K factor can nbe changed within the fixture.

LED under cabinet lights are called pucks. They can be dimmed, are available in four colors, and are controlled by a remote device.

For most of the 20th century, fluorescent lights were used under kitchen wall cabinets in upscale homes. Now it's LED only and also in kitchen and bookcase cabinets in the form of strip lighting. It is known that LED lighting under cabinets kills bacteria which is an added benefit!

LED trims your electric bill. Many manufacturers claim their bulbs last 10,000 to 50,000 hours if the bulb is used three hours a day. That gives you nine to thirty years of use.

Going beyond the recess lights are pendants: chandeliers and wall sconces.

A pendant is a light fixture handing from the ceiling, such as over the kitchen island. Whatever your choice of architecture, you put pendant lights above the island and anywhere else in the kitchen to give light and ambiance. A pendant light hanging above the bath mirror will look elegant. Let elegance be a reflection of you. This serves as a good light for makeup and shaving. Also, a mirror with a switch to light the mirror is a consideration. Research.

The chandelier, on the other hand, shows your opulence. Put a chandelier above the dining room table and breakfast table. If you choose a dome in the entry ceiling, then put in a chandelier. Every dome in your house should have a chandelier unless it obstructs your vision.

Wall Sconces

You cannot put in too many wall sconces, but the ideal location of these fixtures are very limited. Inside, place wall sconces in hallways and on one or both sides of the bath mirror, both sides of the bed and fireplace.

Exterior wall sconces are not for light as much as for ambience. Yard lights mounted on the wall will give you security and keep the yard, especially the pool, well lit. Consider motion lights everywhere in your backyard. Make your backyard light up like daytime with motion lights and direct switching. LED or solar lights in your landscape add a beautiful ambience at night. Light fixtures are a reflection of you.

Smoke Detectors & Exhaust Fans

Smoke detectors must be placed inside every bedroom and outside rooms in hallways. There must also be a detector for carbon monoxide detection. Additionally, this detector is to be placed in a garage which is attached to the house. Use only hard-wired units, not battery operated. This safety requirement can save your life.

Solar lights outside add nice ambience at night. Most come with a rechargeable battery which is easy to maintain, or you can put low voltage lighting, which is costly and not easy to move.

Add ceiling fans wherever you want. Auto charging for the cars, that you may want to buy in the future, is a given.

Install exhaust fans in the bath. Use one for small baths and two for larger baths.

As this author is writing this book, there are search and development companies coming up with electrical and lighting innovations. What is good today may be better tomorrow. All you can do is complete your project and say you did the best with what was available to you at the time.

ELECTRICAL DEFINITIONS

Meter: Glass enclosure in or near the electrical box showing the reading of electricity being used. The electric company will read it physically or remotely from the street which will soon be universal in this country. Some actually read it at their office, remotely. New meter box with provisions for future solar connections.

Main Panel: At the exterior where the power lines enter a box. Generally houses the meter and circuit breakers. Color gray, but it can be painted.

Subpanel: Interior or exterior with additional circuit breakers.

Breakers: Each breaker has a designation to a particular part of the house. Example: a microwave will have one breaker servicing only this unit and is to be labeled so with a Sharpie.

Main Switch: This is the largest of the breakers which, when moved to the off position, shuts off all electrical in the house. Sometimes the fire department will click this in the event of a fire. You can do the same.

Added Note: When installing a new meter box, get one that will have future solar connections. This is a small portion of the box and won't cost much more. If you choose to go solar, this will give you a chance to feed power back to the electrical provider and put money in your pocket—good thing!

LANDSCAPING

Making Your Yard Bloom

Have you seen a well-landscaped front yard? The author has seen very few. In fact, fewer than a dozen.

A nicely landscaped yard is not a hodgepodge with a plant here and a plant there. It has a lawn with real grass or artificial or crushed rocks, as used in areas around Las Vegas and Phoenix, because of the desert element. Only 7.5% of this country is desert, 29% is wilderness, 9% are parks and recreation, 3.5% are rivers and lakes, 11% are farms and orchards, 3% are commercial buildings and downtown areas, 2% are roads, bridges, and highways.

This leaves 35% for cities with houses and landscaping necessary to keep up the value of the home. This author cannot determine what has been built and what is available to build. A guess is that 90% is available to build, which is not part of government land.

If this author is nearly correct, what about the population explosion of this country? Big question! At this time and for the next 100 years, there will be land to build new homes.

Digress a moment. The fictional book, *Rocket Ship Galileo* by Robert A. Heinlein may not be so fictional. The earth became so populated that a huge rocket ship, capable of holding thousands of passengers, became available to ship the over-population to another similar planet. A lottery was drawn and the "lucky ones" got to board the huge spaceship. This was a one-way trip.

The ship sailed to another galaxy, which took up generations of time. Finally arriving, they landed. Everyone gleeful! But to their dismay, this planet could not allow even one passenger off the ship. The planet was overpopulated. In the words of the Prime Minister of France, Emmanuel Macron, "There is not a Planet B."

Let's return to landscaping your house. Good versus bad landscaping.

First Impressions: Create a Wow!

Correct landscaping is essential to increase the value of your home. Educated landscape designers all have one thing in common. If it looks good, it must be good. This is not at all true. What is true is if there is a better layout to do design. These educated designers know species of plants and inorganic materials. Putting lawns, color plants, trees and shrubs where there is space is not the best rule of thumb.

So let's start with the basics: Where do you find the best landscaping design? The answer is on commercial property. Landscape magazine for architects and builders showcases their projects. A lot of thought has gone into these showcase properties.

What do these commercial landscaped properties have in common? Congruity. The pieces all fit together. You can see any commercial property in the world and the landscape is congruent. The developers don't request, they demand. They have value in mind! Only the very best design companies are hired.

Landscape areas are well planned and well maintained. You will not see a different plant here and another there. You will seldom see a small group of one variety placed incrementally.

If these properties have multiple varieties, then they have multiples of each. Never will you see a variety of one or two plants unless the one item is a feature, such as a huge beautiful tree.

When planning your landscape project, begin with how much lawn and how much planted area you wish to have. Once you decide on the lawn, plant it correctly. You can seed the lawn or put in sod. But the preparation is essential.

First, discard any mounds. Mounds have restrictions and they are not proper. A mound looks like you had extra soil and did not dispose of it.

More than 90% of landscapers prep the lawn even with the sidewalks and curbs. This is not proper. Level the soil two inches (not less) than the curb or walkways. The lawn will grow to the height of the sidewalks and curb.

How often do you see this? Drive down your street. You are lucky to see one per block. You can be the one. There are two reasons to do this. First, it looks good. Second, it conserves water. If you put in artificial grass, then the top should be even with the curb.

Trees should be planted away from the house equal to their height. If a tree grows to 35 feet, then plant it 35 feet from the house. Shrubs are not good in front yards. Shrubs are to be planted on the side and rear of the property. Unless you are a celebrity and want privacy. This privacy does not make the front attractive. In Memphis, Tennessee, Elvis Presley's house has shrubs blocking the view, but over 1,000 people a day are let in to see where he lived and was buried.

So let's discuss planted items. A good landscape has a few things in common. We've determined no shrubs in front. Only smaller plants in the front leading to the house. Consider large plants in the very front and reduce the size as they get closer to the house. There can be plants against the house that grow not more than three feet tall when mature.

Never put a tree next to the house. Rats can climb the trees onto your roof and into your attic. Trees are to be planted, as many as you would like, by the curb. This has a downside to consider. Passing cars and trucks may hit the branches so plant away from traffic. There are many trees that will grow above that level but you may have to keep them trimmed until that happens.

Now, what can you do to set off your property landscape so it looks great and better than the others? The answer is rows of the same variety of plants. Repeat the same plant in the row. It may be along the entry or adjacent to the lawn. If you have a distance of 40 feet, then plant the same variety on both sides of the walkway. If you have a walkway crossing the lawn, then you can plant the same variety, or use another variety, as long as it is in the same family. Be congruent.

Caution: Do not plant roses on the side of the walkway. They look good, for sure, but your guests will not appreciate the thorns.

Let's stand back and look at what you have achieved. First thing you see are the rows, which, even if they are smaller plants, stand out. The lawn looks neater than others, and your trees do not impede the beauty of your house. It all adds up to value. Money in your bank!

Pavers Add Curb Appeal

Concrete walkways have given way to pavers. Paving stones are slightly more costly than concrete but add to curb appeal. At this time, developers have not embraced pavers due to the higher costs but you can consider a walkway with pavers if you do not have a larger area.

The paver industry is booming. Replacing asphalt with pavers and laying them from the curb of your house will add a lot of value to your house and will make you feel better for what you have. If you are building new, then pavers are the way to go. Fix yourself a smoothie, go out to the front of your house, admire your pavers, and look at your neighbors' asphalt driveways. Where would you rather live?

Pavers in the backyard? Oh, the backyard! Landscape the backyard. Anything you want to do, since most of your backyard will be landscape, hardscape, or lawn. You do not have to be concerned about curb appeal or resale. You might have a pool Okay, a pool.

Walkways at the rear can also be paver stones. You can choose to do this yourself but you need to know how. Research.

First you need to lay out the walkways. You need to put form boards on both sides and then remove the soil to about six inches deep. Fill in the walkway with about 3" of base soil, which can be purchased from any stone yard. Lay an inch of sand and compact with a hand compactor, available at a home center. Once leveled out, add more sand to the depth of the brick. Compact again and lay the brick. Nice job! If you lose ten lbs. with this job, good. Send the author a thank you bottle of...my collection is growing!

Block Walls

For the best looking block wall, bar none, it's the split-faced block, which goes with any architectural style house from Mediterranean to modern. Don't order a wall built until you look at split-faced block.

Is the backyard large enough to put in an orchard? An orchard is a fun thing. Picking fruit is pleasant but your small animals will also want the fruit. The author says, "Fine, let them have it. There's plenty more." But you can also put repellant under each tree for not a huge cost.

Barbeque

So you want a barbeque? The barbeque has been around since 1940 and for good reason. Place the BBQ at the back of your yard (assuming you don't have twenty acres). The reason: very simple. When guests gather, they will congregate around the BBQ. By putting it away from the house, it will make for a better gathering. If it's close to the house, the guests will pile up and no one will go further into your yard.

If you have wrought iron fences, then shrubs will be your choice. Shrubs planted properly can give you privacy as tall as 10'. Remember, trees that look full today will be only a truck in a few years. You may not think about resale at this time but be proactive. Make your backyard as private as you can so when a prospective buyer looks around, they will love to live there. This book is not about landscaping techniques, varieties, and species of plants, nor types of materials or lighting. It is about landscaping for resale.

Design for Longevity

Landscape the front of your house for resale. No matter if your frontage is large or small, you must follow certain layout guidelines and do them in this order:

1. Level lot as much as you can with no mounds.
2. Place the driveway. If you drive straight in, make the apron at the curb as wide as the building department will allow. If it's a U-shaped driveway, be sure the outside radius is about 100 feet.
3. Make the two aprons as wide as possible. If you plan a circular driveway, it does not have to pass the entry of the house. It could, but it could also be off to one side.

4. Have a walkway from the curb to the front door. Do this no matter how difficult it may be in planning. Guests should never have to walk on your driveway to get to your front door. Envision wide trucks covering your entire driveway and you have 100 guests walking in the mud to get to your front door. It is alright to traverse the driveway with the walkway. In other words, start at the curb, step onto the walkway, cross the driveway (assuming no truck obstruction), and continue to the front door. The walkway must be a minimum of 36" wide. (An even better width is 5').

5. Place your walkway close to the house: a minimum of 24" but 36" would be ideal and enough for all homes. This will allow you to walk around your yard and to the side gates.

6. Design and plant trees placed as far from the front as the mature height. If you have less than 100', then don't plant redwoods.

7. Follow the walkway and driveway (unless your lawn is to the edge) with border plants. Continue border plants. All planted areas next to landscape should be border plants. As said before, never use roses next to the walkway. The first row of border plants, when mature, should not touch the walkways. The second and third row of border plants will add an astonishing interest to your front yard. What to plant? Your local nursery can help you with that!

8. Excavate your lawn to be finished 2" below the curb or walkways. This keeps the sprinkler water and shows a clean manicured look. Happy lawn! Artificial grass looks better at the curb level. If money does not grow on trees, you need a better gardener.

9. A young boy said adults working in the garden is a way for grown-ups to play in the dirt. What you are looking for is a stunning first impression. Create a wow! Mission accomplished.

10. No plants are to be touching unless it's a hedge.

POOLS

Today, pools have no deep ends and therefore, no diving boards. Most pools built today are 4 feet deep. In 4 feet of water, you can swim or stand up. The average person will go into this pool. The big advantage is the heating of a 4' pool is a minimum cost. Plus, there's an added safety factor. There are too many stories of children drowning in pools. A 4' pool is all you need. Also consider a retractable fountain spray. When turned on, it's great for guests and adds a special ambience. The sound is also very soothing.

So your heart is set on a swimming pool. You call pool companies and get their suggestions. A partially good idea. Call as many companies as you feel you need to reach a decision on who to choose to be your contractor. But you may be privy to the most wrong information of your home lifetime. This is how 90% of homeowners approach their pool needs. And this author says that 90% of pools are built incorrectly. They are built like their neighbors, friends, or relatives. This does not make a pool design and construction right for you or for resale.

Most pool companies will suggest that you build a large pool at the far rear of your yard. Wrong. They will suggest a deep end for diving. Wrong. More and more, the permit agencies are not allowing diving boards anyway. A Jacuzzi (Jacuzzi is a brand name for a spa) integrated into the pool space—wrong. But you see it often. That does not make it proper.

Wrong, wrong, wrong. So what is not wrong? During postwar, pools were built and kids drowned. Kids living in the house of the neighbor jumped the fence to play in the pool and died. The author knows of two. That's two too many. So you pledge to always watch the kids as you always watched your babies. Don't discount the neighbors' kids.

Diving went out with the dinosaurs. If you want to go diving, then go to the community pool with a lifeguard watching your kids' safety. If you see a swimmer in distress, are you able to be a life guard? What happens if you are not a good swimmer or temporarily disabled?

Case in point: The best-selling author Charles Krauthammer dove into the deep end of a pool and became a paraplegic for life. Bottom line, no pool should be more than 4' deep. Nearly every hotel built today has a 4' maximum pool depth. Yes, the entire pool is 4' or less.

The placement of the pool is directly related to the resale of your home. Discriminating home buyers know a pool, not close to the house, is not at all acceptable. Situate the pool as close to the house as possible. When standing at the kitchen sink, you want a complete visual of your pool and everyone in it. A buyer will pick up on this. No matter what size your house is, put the pool as close as possible to the house with a good view from the kitchen. The quality of life is the basics. This is more than sound advice.

SPAS

As early as 1939, a trend started to integrate the spa with the pool. Not good. The pool looks good by itself so why put the spa there? Biggest downturn for smaller homes is the energy wasted to heat the spa connected to the pool. Okay, you have unlimited funds, no problem then. But it's still not good for resale. Be alert for the discriminating buyer.

Separate the spa. It looks better and it's far less expensive to run. What size spa? A two-person spa is probably all you need unless your house is larger. Four-bedroom homes need a four-person spa; six or more bedrooms need a four- or six-person spa.

Another reason to put the spa away from the pool is for privacy. Deeper yards have the spa located to be barely seen from the house. This is a good time to research an above-ground spa. Big advantage is you can fill the spa, and after a few usages, drain it completely into the landscape—always having clean water for the next usage. Generally, a two- or four-person spa is good for this. A spa is not more than 2' deep or less at the seat level, which is safer for children. Always use a spa cover when it is not in use. Saves energy and keeps the kids (and animals) out and safe.

Plants are fine around the pool and so much better than a spa. Commercial pools have no planting since guests need to walk around all sides and their spa is not part of the pool. If your pool is round, then plant 3' from the copping about one-third of the circumference. Coping is the hard surface around the pool for walking and should be about 2' wide in order to walk around easily.

Be sure your plants are not deciduous (leaves will die and drop into the pool). This creates a dilemma since the best plant color of your yard should be at or near the pool. Use only non-deciduous flowering plants. (Flowers and leaves that don't drop off during the winter months.) There is nothing worse than having your friends over for a pool party and a wind kicks up and blows the leaves and flowers into the pool. Be proactive.

A first reaction to a good-looking pool is that you must be rich. You are rich. Rich with good ideas. Check out the cost of a retractable fountain. They are not expensive, especially for a basic one. Lighting is a must. Colored lights in the pool and accent lights around the pool, along with yard lights. You want a clear view of your kids at night. Put a light on in the house that shines directly onto the pool.

Water features should not be connected directly into the filtering system. This raises the cost of heating the water due to evaporation, when in operation. Keep the water feature a separate entity. But a retractable fountain is a great crowd-pleaser. The fountain could also come on when filtering. When guests or potential buyers first walk into your yard and see the fountain in the middle of the pool, the "wow" factor clicks in.

Homeowners instinctively have a misconception of pool size at a tremendous cost. In most states, it is illegal to install a diving board. It is best to make your pool smaller, but not too small. The money you save will give you a chance to put in an elevator. Use the elevator every day but use the pool on weekends. After you compare all costs, this will make sense (cents). (See segment on elevators.)

The large pool is a dinosaur for middle-class homes. Large pools are a drain on water usage, gas consumption, and on the operating system. Unfortunately, the same owner installing a water-guzzling pool puts in drought-resistant plants. Go figure.

PATIO

The author just returned from touring a 7,000-square-foot house. Nice because it's new. But the architect did not take into consideration the east sun coming into the house at the backyard between 9 a.m. and 3 p.m., and there was no covered patio which could diminish direct sunlight. The house faced south.

We all know the sun rises in the east and sets in the west, but do we realize south facing is exposure to sun all day? It's not bad if your house faces this direction, but it's the backyard which is of concern.

If at all possible, face the rear of the house to the north. There is no direct sun from the north. Also, plant shade plants in the backyard to create a little paradise. This may be a little exaggeration but if you have a choice of properties in a subdivision, look for north-facing rear yards.

If your rear yard faces the sun, put in a solid covered patio. Contrary to building too large a pool, the larger the patio cover facing the sun, the better. You will enjoy it. Guaranteed!

The patio can be covered by incorporating the structure into the house with support columns. Also, open with a trellis that is so designed to let in only noon-time sun. A properly designed trellis will give shade after 4 p.m. You architect knows.

If you live in an apartment that faces the sun, you can do nothing except close the shades. But this is not your situation. You have a backyard. You must take the time to determine the sun intrusion and plan a patio or trellis accordingly. This is called "being proactive." Take umbrage in the fact that after reading this book, you will know the right thing to do.

FENCES, GATES, AND WALLS

Drive any established street and you will see an array of fences, gates, and walls. In America, fences are a standard way of life. Fences prevent your pets from crossing the roadways. Fences section off the owner's property. Even if you live on a farm, a fence around your house is in order, and I don't mean a chicken-wire fence. This fence will not only keep out intruders but will delineate your property from your neighbors.

If you live in the center of population, you want the fence to section off from your neighbor, but also to give you security from invasion and unwanted larger animals, such as deer and coyotes.

Today, the cities are sprawling into formerly uninhabitable regions. Fences are a MUST. Chain link fences came about in the 19th century. This fence, five or six feet tall, was the answer for more than two centuries. Relatively inexpensive, as well as strong and durable, it is not the best for resale value.

Then along came the wrought iron fence. Wrought iron is much more expensive but very attractive. Chain link fencing is constructed onsite. Iron fences must first be fabricated in a workshop, then delivered to the site and installed with welded or screw-in attachments. Chain link has one style but iron design is up to the buyer. Both fences have something in common. They are see-through. Also to mention are clear glass or plastic for a more contemporary look, but used primarily on decks and patios (small areas).

What color to paint the wrought iron fence? Chain link comes pre-finished galvanized which will hold up well for forty years unless it is in the wetter regions, which will reduce the lifespan to thirty years. After that time, rust will appear, therefore, to keep it looking good, cover it with galvanized paint.

Chain link fences have lasted for more than a century. You may have photos of your great grandfather installing the chain link fence that exists on your property today. The only thing that was most likely needed was repair. Repair from fallen trees or from being washed out in a flood.

Wrought iron fences do not have this history. But there is no reason iron would not last as long or longer.

Back to the color to paint your iron fence. Not white or near white. In a matter of a few years, rust will appear. This will make you look bad when you have your heart set on increasing your property value. The bottom line is to paint them black.

There is another big reason—obscurity. Look at a black-painted iron fence. Squint your eyes and the fence will disappear. This is why this author will be selling 60,000 books. Wishful thinking!

Iron fences are not to be placed between property lines—only at the front and side of a roadway. If you have a corner lot then fence two sides. Where your property abuts the neighbor, then a solid fence or wall is in order.

A solid fence, in the past, consisted of wood—either fir or redwood. Problem was, after forty years, the fence became shabby and looked out of place. Painting and repair helped. Start with a wood fence and change it later if you live long enough in your house. Vinyl or composite fencing came on the market around 1975. These fences will last the lifetime of your house. Explore your options.

So you have money left over after remodeling. Wall your property. There are not many options when building a wall. It is to be cinderblock. Fences do not always require building approval. A wall must have an engineering's blessing by the building department to be approved. This will mean inspection of the foundation of the wall. Do it right. Get approvals. There are restrictions on walls. Take a proposed plan to the department for a pre-plan check on the walls before you call for contractors' bids. The department does not care about the materials you use—only the structural value.

There are many options of materials to build your wall. The author recommends a split face block. This block will blend with any architectural design, from contemporary to traditional to whatever.

Gates must be at least 36" wide in order to accommodate trash cans. Gates should be self closing. Put a hold-open device when doing gardening. Use a digital key pad built into the gate which will open with your code, and add a key lock. You don't think much about security until you are away from the house for a long period of time and someone enters your property. Be proactive.

STORAGE

Life Uncluttered

You cannot have enough storage space. It is said that if you want to double your storage space, then get rid of half of your stuff. Okay, not an option!

Storage in the garage is one place to start. Put in cabinets with doors since this will look better from the street. If your garage is large enough, then use full-height cabinets, but if space is limited, then use floating cabinets where the car can park underneath.

You have factored in closets and wardrobes into your room plans, but what more can you do? If you have a gable roof, the answer is the attic. With contemporary design there is no attic space. Noted! A gable roof with a pitch of 6 in 12 has adequate space for extra storage. It is best to have an approved staircase leading to the attic. If this is not possible, then a fold-down ladder will suffice. Section off a portion for storage with access doors to the balance of the attic which houses the heating ducts.

A window is not necessary unless it will add to the architectural value. Construct this area as you would any room with air-tight openings to make it rodent and bug proof. This area will give you lots of storage, even if it's only 25% of the attic.

Storage under the stairs is to be treated with the same enclosure as the attic (if you have the space and the stairs).

Another option is the armoire, a freestanding cabinet to put in the bedrooms as an extension of your closets for clothes. Generally, this is a nice piece of furniture and works well for guests. Also, it can be used to supplement the master bedroom storage needs.

A storage cabinet above the toilet will hold most bath items. This author does not recommend a medicine cabinet. They are good for small items but a freestanding mirror is the trend today with your tamper-proof medicine containers stored in the cabinet drawers. Be sure that at least one drawer is 6" deep to hold rolls of toilet paper.

Drawers under the bed are an option since beds are now higher from the floor. Built-in bookcases that accommodate books should be enclosed with doors. Open shelves are not recommended since the doors only cost about 20% more, and glass fronts that are lighted or solid are more attractive (plus they are earthquake-proof). Compare with store-bought units as long as it will fit the space.

A linen cabinet near the laundry room or in the hall is a given. The unit should not be more than 18" deep. You can put a folded towel in a 12" deep cabinet. Anything deeper and your items will get lost in the back and never used.

Do not put storage in the yard unless for gardening tools. Boxes, etc. collect pests. Try to stay away from sheds unless they are attached to the house and sealed so they are pest proof.

Then there is the basement, which again, should be completely sealed off from pests.

Proper closet arrangement will give you maximum storage. The walk-in closet should have double hanging poles (70% of space), single-hanging (10%), and open shelving or cabinets (20%) for shoes, sweaters, hand bags, and other folded items. Additionally, there needs to be some space for open shelves above all hanging sides of the closet.

FIREPLACES AND TELEVISIONS

Pause a Moment

A fireplace is a must-have. At least one unit. If your house is small, you at least need a small fireplace. Even if you've never used a fireplace, put one in. Every house should have one. It's a resale thing. If you don't have one at the time, down the line, when you sell the house and every potential buyer asks, "Where is the fireplace?" you will regret not having one. Don't go through this agony. Be proactive!

For 3,000 years, the fireplace was used to keep the resident warm. And in many cases, for cooking and warming water. Today, it's only for aesthetics but will also warm a small area the size of a guest house: a 36" fireplace will heat a 650-square-foot guest house about two degrees an hour.

If you only have one fireplace, put it in the family room below the wall TV.

The second unit goes in the master bedroom opposite the bed with the TV above.

The third unit goes into the living room if you have one. If there is no TV above the mantel, then put in a large mirror or artwork.

The fourth fireplace is outside on the patio and the fifth and final unit goes in the sitting room nearest the master bedroom with a TV above. Also, the guest house should have one in the living room with a TV above, and one in the bedroom.

No fireplace? You have a middle-class home with lower class amenities.

Okay, so we missed the dining room. Well it's because times have changed. During the colonial years, the fireplace was in the main room which was the dining room/living room, and in many cases, the sleeping room.

You may have noticed that these are not the colonial years. We are beyond colonizing. So do not put a fireplace in the dining room. With that said, William Randolph Hearst built the Hearst Castle with a fireplace in the dining room, so large that you could stand in it. Purely Hearst fantasy, but a huge hit with dining guests, and now, the touring crowd.

The evolution of time changed the dining room use from one of leisure to dining-only. The author stayed in a fabulous house owned by relatives in Paris, France. Uncle married a French woman while he was deployed there during the war. The fireplace was nice, but not extravagant, and the dinner lasted two hours. If you are to sit through a leisurely two-hour dinner, then why not have a fireplace?

Today dinner is served family-style. Pass it around. Does anyone want more? No time to enjoy the ambience of the fireplace. Thus, don't put one in this room.

Most fireplaces should have provisions for a TV above. If you don't want a TV, then put in the provisions and cover it with a picture or mirror, including in the bathrooms. Las Vegas hotel rooms, which are the most advanced in the world, have TVs in the bathrooms; but lately, have removed them with remodeling. Sometimes it is impossible to keep up!

The fireplace made of brick and stone has given way to a prefabricated unit. You have seen homes burnt to the ground with only the chimney standing intact. This is because brick does not burn. But the brick fireplace was so costly that only one was used in any house.

Today, we do not have to fear the house burning down. Fireplaces and chimneys are constructed the same as the rest of the house. The chimney is double-wrapped through the roof.

The chimney, exposed to the exterior, is a style that fits with the décor of your house. But with one added feature: a smoke arrester. This prevents embers from a nearby fire to enter the atmosphere and cause a fire elsewhere. But this also has diminished the birds from doing their duty down your chimney and into the fireplace. They also will nest in an open chimney. How they attach to the duct wall is a mystery.

Next, make your fireplace surround-safe while complying with department regulations. The surround must have non-combustible tile or stone, set 6" on either side, 12" above to the mantle—if you have one—and an 18" hearth. This will comply and look great. This can also be achieved by a glass enclosure.

Today, many have doors. If you have doors, it will be allowed to use only fire-rated drywall surround. This is good for a cleaner look. Research. You can research various finishes that will fit the façade of your fireplace.

You must have a remote device to regulate the unit. There are two types: one you hold to regulate the fire and one that turns on and off completely with just a touch. Larger units work better with doors open.

The surround of the main fireplace should be directly related to the size of your house and the quality of your decorating. If it's modern, use stacked stone or wood trim, with or without a wood mantle. If it's Mediterranean, use precast stone. If you have a traditional house, then use stone surrounded with wood trim and a wood mantle, also with wood trim. Reflect your radiance.

You can purchase individual items, such as Caesarstone or tile or get a prefab unit online. Much like your kitchen and bath, the main fireplace is a reflection of you.

Televisions can be connected to speakers for surround sound in the ceiling. Watching *Star Wars* with surround sound puts you closer to the action. Be a person of good judgement.

INDOOR PLANTS

All the plants need not be real

Every major room must have a plant. The plants you choose are a mirror image of you. Some rooms, such as the kitchen, family room, dining room, master bedroom, master bath, office, conservatory, sun room, patio and entry should have colored plants. All other rooms such as the other bedrooms, powder room, living room, study, library and any room not frequented are to have non-colored plants.

Not to worry if all plants are not real. With the artificial look-alike plants of today, you can use them anywhere, except the kitchen. It is not the kind of plant itself, it's the purpose of the plant. Put artificial plants wherever you cannot continuously attend to them. The bottom line here is ambience.

Larger artificial plants look great. Consider a six- or seven-foot-tall tree, but not very wide, up against a wall with a larger mirror behind it. This will give an impression of a very nice house. What more can you ask?

To get an idea of what plants add to a room, turn to any furniture or accessory catalog that comes in the mail. On every page showing a room vignette, you will see a plant. Copy this, since these room designers have done their homework for you.

The pot should generally be about 1/3 the height of the plant. Thus, a six-foot-tall tree should have a pot of about two feet.

Put potted plants in the living room, family room, bedrooms, dining room, office, conservatory, sun room, patio and entry. The smaller the room, the smaller the plant. Thus, the smaller the pot. Don't overlook woven baskets—any size, anywhere.

The color and style are to blend with your interior decoration. Consider not using terra cotta pots since they are more for exterior use. Black or white usually will fit in. Every house should have a money plant. Bookshelves need to have plants that flow over the top. Invest in nice, rich-looking containers. Bring outdoor plants inside to reduce pollutants and for your quality of life and personal style.

Once again, the objective is to create a good first impression. Make a statement with your indoor plants.

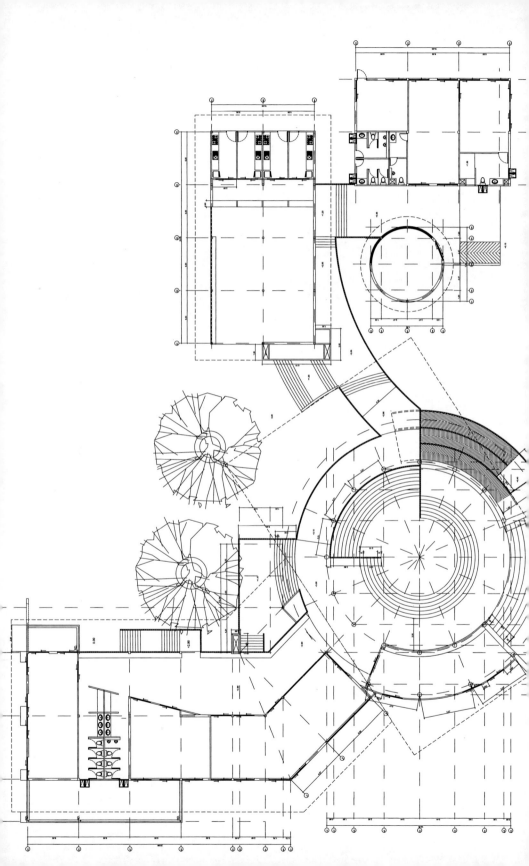

4

It's Your Domain:
Building a Team

It's Your Domain: Building a Team

FINDING AN ARCHITECT

Building a Team

It's easy to find the architect just right for you. There are three types of architects:

1. One who just draws lines. This is not a good choice, since they will not be helpful with guiding you.

2. The opposite is the one who is adamant you do things their way and won't budge from their suggestions. They are also not helpful to your end product. Don't be talked out of what you really know and what you want.

3. The third will draw lines, be open to your suggestions and requests, and will give you advice base on their experience with your type of project. This type of architect is best for you to reach your goals.

Where do you find an architect? Ask your Realtor or someone who has had a good experience. Ask for references. Call those references and ask the leading question: "How do they fit into your needs?" Then ask the building department to tell you of their experience with this architect. The leading question here is: Are their plans usually complete and do they meet department requirements when they are first submitted?

When plans are complete, use this checklist to ensure you will get department approval and clarity for you to submit it to the contractor. The contractor will be impressed with your knowledge.

- You will want to know their fees and what is provided.
- You will want a preliminary plan drawn first for a separate fee. A preliminary plan shows both the existing floor plan and the proposed floor plan.

Questions to your architect should include:

1. Will the plan show what you want?
2. Your ideas and notes.
3. What will changes cost?
4. Who will be paying for the printing of plans and what is the cost?

No project should start without a preliminary plan. Be steadfast on this. What you don't want is a complete set of plans drawn at this early stage. Before getting in too deep, you need to know if you can afford the project. Will it fit in your budget? The preliminary plan consists of only a floor plan and site plan, if one is needed. Be sure to refer back to the department for setback requirements.

The preliminary plan shows the existing structure and proposed structure and what is to be added and removed, all on one 24" by 36" sheet. What you want is a clear picture of your dream. At this time, it is not necessary for details, such as electrical layout and cabinet elevations. Your preliminary plan should address the needed exterior changes to meet your expectations.

Study the initial preliminary plan and make changes as you desire. Have the architect redraw the preliminary as you request, but be careful here. Some architects will not want to do it your way. Some think they know better. Good. Listen to what is presented but do it your way, as Frank Sinatra did.

At the same time, listen to what the architect has to say and weigh it accordingly. This is a major understanding for you and you just want to get it right. The world is full of wrong turns and dead ends, but with a map of proper direction, you will see the light. There will be few details on the preliminary plan, but they will all come to light later in the project. The objective is to have a pleasant experience!

Now you are done with the preliminary. What are you to do next? Call a contractor—someone who will sit down to discuss the overall project. Provide the contractor with the appliance and plumbing quotes. This is the time to determine if the project you envision will come to fruition before investing in complete plans. Stop here.

There are contractors who offer a service of preliminary plans. They will draw it themselves, hire someone to draw it for you, or refer someone they work with who is good. All contractors are associated with designers and architects. A good contractor, coupled with a good architect, will make your dream home come true.

Next, you give the building department the valuation. They will give you a plan-check-fee amount and a permit-fee amount based upon your valuation. The valuation may be increased by the plan checker. The total of these fees are part of your budget. This may vary after plans are drawn, but you are now only looking for a budget.

You now have three items helping you get a determined budget.

When plans are complete, use this checklist to ensure you will get departmental approval and clarity for you to submit it to the contractor:

Items to be Part of the Completed Plans

1. Floor plan showing new walls.
2. Electrical plan showing every individual item from recess lights to outlets.
3. Door and window schedule.
4. Site plan, fully dimensioned, showing drainage and landscape.
5. Vicinity plan.
6. Foundation plan showing proposed and existing foundation.
7. Demolition plan.
8. Elevations showing roofing, new and existing to remain.
9. General notes for clarity.
10. Green notes.
11. Energy notes.
12. Fire and safety codes.
13. Cross-sections showing insulation, minimum two sections.
14. Cabinet elevations showing appliances.
15. Eve details.
16. Staircase details.
17. Any excavation.
18. Lot coverage.
19. Index to find sheets easily.
20. Interior and exterior remodeling details.

You are now becoming "an expert" and you should be feeling pretty good about your project. It's time to find a contractor. Know who is a good contractor? Let's start with the last item first, the contractor's management fee. The fixed fee is 20% to cover supervision, overhead, and profit. Gone is the 5% contingency factor, since most material houses and subcontractors have similar pricing. Contingency is not a factor, but contractors have additional discounts available for early payments and take advantage of sales discounts.

A sales person for a construction company may be good for you but some charge 10% and then seldom, if at all, come around again. A salesperson generally works for a larger company. If your project and budget is large enough, then this will be the way to go.

You should provide 24" x 36" full size plans. Digital plans from the emails may be lost in clarity and may result in an inaccurate final quote.

It goes without saying that the contractor must know how to read plans. If you follow the previous check list, the contractor will have fewer questions. Request that the contractor bid the project from the plan, as is, with a list of questions for you and the architect.

There are more than 250,000 general contractors in this country. You need to only find one. Not that difficult. There are many places to look, but one is the material supplier. Suppliers know who has been naughty or nice. In other words, who pays their bills on time? Other references may come from friends and neighbors with whom they have done business.

The leading information to obtain is: How accessible is the contractor for the job meetings? If a person is on time for the initial appointment, then there is a good chance they will be on time in the future, especially on time with completion. Their appearance or the car or truck they drive is not of importance. Sam Walton made a billion with Walmart while driving an older beat-up pickup truck!

Now some history: About the time after the Revolutionary War, there were no contractors. There were no licensed designers, but there were architects. You could not call a contractor to quote your project because there were none. Buildings were not built that way. They were built by self-proclaimed architects. The architects would draw plans and then oversee the project, as well. One person. Seems simple: architect, draftsman, engineer, contractor, and supervisor—all in one.

The architect would have a number of employees doing multiple tasks. You had to trust this person implicitly since there was no one above them. There was always a shortage of architects during this period.

Today, following the many catastrophes in this country, we now have a shortage of contractors. Lots of lawyers, but not enough contractors.

FINDING A CONTRACTOR

Consideration Goes a Long Way

At your initial meeting with a contractor ask: "What do you think of the plan?" Their comments will give you an indication of needed help during the construction process. Ask about their workload and schedule, when can work start, and how long until completion? Ask what they think of plans based on their experience. It's a good idea not to have the architect at the initial meeting.

Sometimes, if a contractor has no suggestions at the initial meeting, they will be looking for costly change orders. Any cost, not part of the original cost breakdown, is a change order. The amount, after you agree, will be added to the request for payment later as a change order.

Avoid change orders with good planning. Complete plans include all structural details and schedules (one is a window and door schedule spelling out each unit and is key to the plans). Change orders are always part of construction. You will want something on the site to add. A change order is required.

You will want your contractor to be good. You need to be a good customer. The contractor will supply you with a progressive payment plan. This is to alert you when payments are due. Make payments on time (per payment plan). Don't request something for nothing, thinking you have the power of the checkbook.

Keep in mind not to complain. When you see something is not right, simply ask for it to be corrected. Be a concerned customer, not a habitual complainer. Do not repeat the same text, email, or phone call. This goes a long way with the contractor and the workmen. Be pleasant to deal with and you will be rewarded in the end. You may want to hire the contractor for future remodeling. Will your phone call be answered? Will your good fortune be continued?

Most contractors fail as business people within the first ten years. This statistic is super important to you. In order to keep a cash flow, they rob Peter to pay Paul. When work stops, they stop. When they do get a project signed up, they start with a shortage of cash. Few contractors are business savvy. They know the trade, but not the business end. Contractors working alone have little or any time for job costing, updating statements, or general accounting. Only hire a contractor with a team.

You must be proactive. If you check out three contractors and they come highly recommended, then you are starting correctly. If one comes in with an extremely low bid, chances are you are going to be the one holding the bag—and the money bag will be empty! You may get the job done but what about the lack of craftsmanship, timely meeting appointments, paying the workmen, and workers compensation insurance—in the event a workman falls off the roof? The big item is since you have not ever hired a contractor before, you may experience the "don't bother me" syndrome.

You call to ask why no one has showed up to work and get the "don't bother me" answer. It's always that they are doing the best they can, be patient and bring semblance to your project. Be on the offense without being offensive.

They may be doing the best they can but the problem is they do not have the financial resources. The only way they can finish your job is to rob Peter to pay Paul (in this case, your project).

This author suggests you become pragmatic from the start. Know that a quote that is substantially less than another quote means you will be walking on thin ice.

So you say that the minute after I sign the contract I will hire a lawyer? Then you are putting yourself in an aspirin syndrome. Have fun! No, it's better to step back and look at this scenario objectively. When it looks too good to be true, it usually is too good to be true.

Would you buy a discount flight knowing the pilot is an alcoholic and the plane could crash? Maybe you will survive. Case closed. What you do will show up in your bank account balance.

SKYLIGHTS AND SOLAR PANELS

Eye Sore

If you have a room without windows, such as a laundry or powder room, you may opt for a skylight. But consider this: even with a skylight, you will most likely flip the light switch because you are accustomed to turning on lights when entering any room. So what good is a skylight?

What is not good is the appearance of the skylight from the exterior of your house, especially from the front. A house without skylights as seen from the front or backyard is a cleaner look. The same holds true for solar panels.

Skylights basically come round (solar-tube) or square. The solar-tube is available in various sizes, but the small sizes should generally suffice. The advantage is that a pipe between the ceiling and the roof is all that is required. These are completely insulated and cost less. If you want a skylight then this is a good investment. Option? Either round or square will work fine.

A square skylight lets in less light, needs to be cleared on top of the roof and needs a built-in insulated chase between the ceiling and the roof. This can be costly. The advantage is that it has a ventilating lid at the roof line with a screen operated by a hand crank or remote-controlled in the room at the light switch.

Either skylight is available with an artificial light for darkness, which is also controlled at the switch.

Skylights were the rage between 1950 and 2000, but into the turn of the century, more skylights have been removed than installed. Skylights will, from now on, be used in middle-class homes, not lower or upper class. Think about it. Think about the enigma, the lower class cannot afford them and the upper class does not want them.

The downside is what you spend so much money on a skylight and see bright, natural light coming in from the window. As with covering the ceiling with too many lights, if it becomes too much you have little control other than shading the window and not allowing a view out—disconcerting!

You cannot light a staircase enough, both in daytime with or without a skylight, and at night with motion lights. The stairs are the most dangerous part of the house. Be proactive and consider a skylight or motion lights. Be safe or be sorry! Of course a window at the head of the stairs is all you need during daylight.

This author is not a fan of skylights but is a very big fan of safety. Best left to your research and consideration. Let this author know your opinion.

Plant a Tree on Your Roof

This author is also not a big fan of solar panels, but solar, in one form or another, is the future. Energy that this globe wastes by not tapping into the sun's rays is gargantuan. For thousands of years, this free energy has gone unabated—like water down the drain. We are capturing the sun's rays only now with solar panels on residential homes. The upside of solar panels is that they cut the cost of your gas and electric bills. This is good and is the selling point of solar installation companies, a few developers, and some state officials.

But do they save on gas and electric use? Yes they do. Some to the extent that you may feed back to the companies your unused solar power. It's like making a business of it!

Let's settle down. It's not at all that exhilarating. The investment does not pencil out! Does the investment into a solar panel system really save or bring you money? In this time and age, the answer is a formative "no."

If you have panels over your roofing, it can be costly to fix roof leaks. The panels, after a period of time, must be replaced. When it comes time to re-roof, the cost of removing the panels and reinstalling them is higher than you anticipated. Therefore, the cost of panels never exceeds the gain you see on your utility bill. Never! Never! It's a negative cost factor ratio.

It would be great if the panels last forever but they don't. Why? The technology does not exist. But let's say you break even. If you do, then you lose because of the unsightliness. This goes beyond saving panels. Homes with solar panels sell for less due to their unsightly appearance. You cannot avoid this since you must place panels facing south. South facing has sun all day and that is why panels must be situated on this side of the roof.

If the south direction is at the front of your house, it makes for an unsightly view from the street. Think of it this way: We all love trees. Why not plant a tree on top of your roof? Answer: Out of place!

Panels are placed on the roof over the roofing after installed. There is a space, all so small, that attracts rats. Rats love this environment and over time will find a way into your attic. You can rat poison the area but that poison that kills the rats will kill other animals who feed on them—such as your cats or the neighbors' cats. It's not a good scenario.

Homes that feature solar panels for sale sell for less. Not for the rats (most do not know about this problem), but for lack of curb appeal.

You choose the best roofing for your house and cover it with solar panels? Go figure! Solar companies will give you time payments, some without interest. Gotcha!

The answer to this dilemma will be in technology. Today there are few options to pencil out the negative of the solar problem. Tesla Company has come up with solar tiles. Solar tiles will replace roofing and give solar usage. It's not known yet if this will be cost effective but it is a possible solution. Tesla is wrestling with this and hopes to know more soon. Stay tuned.

Tesla tiles are the beginning of the next evolution for solar. In the coming years, solar innovation will be a thing of the future. It will come as stucco used to cover exterior walls, slow but sure.

How to put your money down the drain? Invest in solar panels. With that said, foldable solar panels, when hiking, can save your life since they will activate your emergency call. Panels have a problem of spontaneous combustion. Walmart installed panels on many buildings, some of which caused fires. This could happen to your home installation. Walmart has filed a law suit. Be proactive.

INSULATION AND SOUND PROOFING

Green Living is Better Living

This chapter will deal with soundproofing of floors, walls, laundry noise, music rooms, and toilets.

Until the 20th century, soundproofing was not a consideration. Architects dismissed sound transmission as a way of life. Then along came insulation in 1935. Monsanto invented fiberglass material, and when used in walls, it not only insulated them against the elements but also insulated them against sound. It took ten more years before houses installed insulation. But only 3% used this new innovation when building new homes.

Only 6% of houses built from 1945 to 1970 were built with insulation. But in 1970, insulation use became the norm. The departments required insulation in walls and ceilings but not yet in the floor. One decade later, insulation was also required in floors. But this was the time concrete slab floors were the preference of the engineer and the discriminating home buyer.

The purpose of insulation was to keep out the elements, but an added value was sound proofing. Insulation did not keep out road noise, it reduced it. See the irony of this all. We did not have freeway or highway noise since these were not the noisy roadways. Insulation, alone, does not prevent sound from impregnating—it reduces it.

Okay, now you know insulation reduces sound somewhat. Stucco also insulates against sound. Stucco was the finish of last resort for homes built in the 19th and 20th centuries. Builders resisted stucco saying it would not hold up during extreme cold temperatures. Stucco is not the total layers on the house. Stucco is the 1/8" finish over two layers of cement. But we call this total thickness stucco as we call the 1/10" Formica laminated on ¾" plywood Formica.

Most of the southern states, including Texas, resisted stucco. Houses were built of brick or wood siding in Texas and most of the Midwest.

Brick is better insulation than stucco, all will agree. So much for the finished house, but what about the addition? It's costly to tear down brick to add on. Today, Texas has embraced stucco as a cost factor. Brick façade front and stucco balance at the house. Best of two worlds.

Lath and plaster also are a sound barrier of some sort. About the time when chicken wire was used for exterior cement, plaster was applied over 3/8" x 1 3/8" wood lath for all interior walls and ceilings. This was the wall finish for three centuries until 1945. The application was used in every house built from the time after log houses to 1950. Nothing in the building industry is 100%. But lath and plaster of interior walls during this period in time comes very close. Plaster and stucco will crack. Guaranteed. Vinyl paint will cover most stucco cracks and drywall tape will cover plaster cracks.

Ever Changing

Then along came drywall. Half-inch drywall was first used in St. Louis, postwar. Homes still used plaster, but eventually moved to drywall. Additions to existing plastered homes were dry walled with half-inch drywall material.

Unfortunately, this is not as soundproof, and houses with exterior siding and interior plaster or half-inch drywall were not close to being fire resistant. When houses burned, they burned down completely due to the wood lath.

Then along came 5/8" drywall, originally used for one-hour fire rating (it takes one hour to burn through). This gave time to save portions of the house from completely burning down. Today, all houses are built entirely with 5/8" fire-rated drywall. The added bonus is insulation. The thicker the drywall, the better the insulation.

In 1970, when the majority of building departments required insulation in the walls and ceiling for energy savings, it also gave the home additional sound proofing. It was shortly thereafter, around 1985, when the departments required the floors also to be insulated. Floor insulation requirements lasted until concrete slabs were the way of builders.

Today, room additions are primarily added to wood floors with concrete slabs. Therefore, part of the house is wood and part concrete floors. This was a concern for many with two-floor constructions, but this went out the window with composite floor covering. Composite flooring has a soft pad under to make it soft to walk on, no matter if wood or concrete is under an added insulation.

In 2017, building departments required thicker wall and ceiling insulation for energy savings, which also increased the sound proofing. In 2000, walls were required to be covered with ½" plywood which also added to insulation and soundproofing. Homes began the transformation of just a structure to a better place to live, amounting to greater value, energy savings, strength of structure, and fire proofing.

Additional sound proofing, over and above what is required, are these two items: sound proof insulation, which is a denser material, and also sound proof drywall. Add these to a music room if your future artist plays the drums or if you want no sound between two rooms, such as a bath and bedroom.

Make it Happen

Solid core doors are better. You already have dual pane window glass which has a high energy and sound resistance. You can build your home next to train tracks and not hear a sound. Sorry—not guaranteed.

Nothing is more annoying than to hear the toilet flush while sleeping in a bed. The best remedy is to put the toilet in a compartment which is an enclosed room with a door. If this can't be done, separate the bath and bedroom with a sound proof wall. This consists of a solid core door, sound proof insulation and sound proof drywall. The objective is to sleep tight.

Some homes are built facing a busy thoroughfare. Sound-proof windows (double pane), sound-proof drywall, and insulation are the answer. This does cost more, but later you will wish you had incorporated it.

Sound proofing around the laundry room requires the same construction. But the laundry should not be placed near the sleeping areas. It is best to put the laundry nearest the kitchen and away from bedrooms. The exception is the bedroom used for the live-in housekeeper, which is also nearest the kitchen.

If you have the bucks for this, then the author is open to a personal loan.

If you plan upfront for a loud music room for one of your children who plays the drums, then it is necessary to install acoustic walls and ceiling. The same as for other areas, plus the ceiling is to be acoustic tile.

You can find acoustic tile that will blend with the décor of your house. After the kid moves out, you can use this room for moments alone. The music acoustics will be soothing. Make it happen.

Not all municipalities have incorporated these requirements. But soon, they will be universal.

PESTS

They Were Here Before You Were

Pests. No, not your neighbors. It's the furry animals and insects that invade your house. No house in America is immune. Guaranteed. You can take that to the bank. These animals and insects invading your house were here long before you were. Their ancestors were in this country before the Conquistadors, before Columbus, and the Native Americans—perhaps a million years before.

Rats litter twice a year. If you leave your attic or under-house unattended, then you will have two families living off your wires. Rats have been known to chew wires in walls and attics causing fires. They chew on wires to sharpen their teeth. If two wires mix together it causes a spark and there goes your house.

Rats are everywhere. In 2019, Los Angeles City Hall had an infestation of rats. Like oceans and mountains, they are not going away. They are not prevalent on Mars. The next spaceship leaving will be...only God knows.

So you must confront the problem. You don't care if they live elsewhere, but not in your home. You want them out. Even if you live in a vault, they may come in through the ventilation shaft.

Rats and ants have something in common. They wander. They keep looking over an expansive area to find their way through. If you have an attic—and most people do—then they will find their way in. You cannot cover every minute hole.

In Europe, the plague from 1347 to 1351 was spread by rats. It took years to discover the reason people died. You drift off to sleep knowing that if the plague comes back, you are living at ground zero.

Then there were millions, today you need to only deal with a few.

Rat traps are not the only answer. Poison will do the job. Most homeowners feel that putting out poison in the attic or under the house once or twice is enough. Wrong. Rats are known to eat a lot of bait which will allow the next family to infest. You must put lots of bait out and check it once a month. Home centers have a section of various types. Traps are to get one or two. You need a lot of bait.

Then the ants will come. You may see a stream of ants going up the wall and into your attic. These ants are cleaning out the carcasses of the dead rats. Let them do their job. They will be preoccupied and not go into your kitchen.

If ants are in your kitchen or any room, then a fogger is in order. Set off the fogger, leave the house for twenty-four hours, and the ants will be gone, along with any other insects, such as spiders and most termites. When the ants return, another fogger is in order.

Keep the Vermin Out

You can minimize the rodent infestation by proper landscaping. It's nice to have ivy and other close-grown plants for appearance, but they do collect rats. Bottom line, no ivy whatsoever. If your neighbors have these plants then try to encourage their removal. It's best for both of you.

This author has it all figured out: Put a raccoon in the attic and an ant eater in the backyard. Problem solved.

Termites are everywhere, in every house in America. Some houses have a few, some have many, and others, a total infestation. Eradicate termites today and they will come back tomorrow, unfortunately. Termite companies cannot rid the subterranean type. They are in the ground. They come out once a year for about two weeks. They can be vacuumed but you cannot reach the nest.

Someone with a new house screams when a termite is noticed. A new house! How can this be? Simple. The termites, although generally only a few, hitched a ride in the lumber that was delivered to your site.

If you have a new house, the termites will increase. If you have an older house, the termites are already there. You tear down a wall and there they are. But they are not the end of the world.

The author will assure you, unequivocally, that termites will not (99% of the time) affect the structural integrity of your house. During your lifetime, termites will not be a major problem.

Remodelers have torn down exterior walls to find many studs and plates infested with termites. But the wall held up just fine over the years. No question. This is the time to eradicate the termites and replace the infested wood and move on.

You can't avoid termites, but you can make your home less welcoming. As you put a fence around your house, so to speak, against the termites. First is the concrete slab floor. It's not a 100% barrier, but it comes close. Go around your house. Determine your floor line by measuring down from a window. Transfer that measurement to the exterior. The soil must be eight inches below this line (floor level) and one inch below if concrete.

Termites don't crawl up the wall more than a few feet. They enter at ground level and infest a few feet up the wall, generally only two feet. Stucco is not a barrier.

If the process is not feasible due to your landscape, then put in a termite wall. This is four inches thick and runs wherever you have this situation.

Whatever you do will show up at the bank.

PIPES AND FILTERS

Copper Versus Galvanized

What makes your house run? Pipes are what makes your house run. Filters are what makes your house run efficiently.

If I were a betting person, I would bet that you would not look for a chapter on filters in this book. Filters have been overlooked by homeowners. The installers do not educate you on filter change. Follow instructions that come packaged with items.

A clogged auto air or oil filter will reduce your gas mileage significantly. When you go in for an oil change, the technician checks the filter and if you need a replacement, then you, without question, replace it.

Not so with filters in your home. The main filter is in your new FAU (Forced Air Units). If you are living in your house full time then every unit's filters must be changed or cleaned twice a year. The best time to do this is the beginning of summer and the beginning of winter. Changing or cleaning them twice a year will be all you need. Generally, they are located at the intake in the hallway or at the unit itself.

Be proactive. When the technician is installing, ask about where to change filters and where they are located. Cleaning them with a hose twice a year will be all you need to do. But if, when spraying, the filter comes apart, replace it. All filters are standard in size and available at home building centers.

Filters in the home became part of the appliances when they hit the market. Today, there is no way to avoid a filter. Some filters can be cleaned and others must be replaced. If your refrigerator has an ice maker or filtered water, then the filter must be replaced once a year.

These filters are not easy to come by. The home building centers do not sell them since there are too many different sizes and varieties and, believe it or not, there is not a big market. Therefore, valuable shelf space does not allow a display. But wherever appliances are sold, assuming they sell your appliance brand, you can get a filter. You can order online. For the refrigerator, have one spare in your household.

The instant hot water dispensers have filters too. Some need replacement and others just need to be cleaned out. The replacement filter is under the sink. Simply unscrew the filter and install the new one. If you use this often, then replace it often—about every six months.

Instant hot units must be cleaned at the spout. Unscrew the filter by hand or use a wrench. About once or twice a year, unscrew and let the water flow into the sink which will allow sediment to escape. If a lot of gunk comes out, this will tell you to clean out this filter more often.

Your water looks clear and pure, so why do pipes clog? The answer is sediment. Sediment has been around for a billion years. Sediment is how rocks were formed. It will not go away. As much as the municipal water department keeps your water flowing healthfully, there is still going to be sediment. Therefore, there needs to be filters.

If you are building a new house, you need not worry about the water, drain and sewer lines. These lines will be copper, cast iron, or ABS plastic. Not a problem since sediment will have a hard time clinging to the walls of these pipes. (Still can't get away from using filters.)

But what about remodeling an older house? Good pipes are essential to move forward. Or perhaps you are building a new house where another was torn down. Pipes! Prior to the war, homes were built with sewer lines to the street. Primarily, the pipes were clay. Clay pipes come in sections of about ten feet and the joints filled and compressed with a rope/resin. This held up for about ninety years until the tree roots spread their way into these connections looking for water. (Seems as if they had a mind of their own.)

Unfortunately, the roots clogged the inside of the sewer pipes. The massive intrusion is more than a sewer rooter can handle without breaking the pipe itself. Replace these sewer lines with non-evasive material.

About the turn of the 20th century, galvanized water pipes were used. To get water to the shower was a godsend. Unfortunately, galvanized pipes did not hold up with time. But it got worse. South Korea sent a zillion galvanized pipes to us at a ridiculously low price which we could not refuse. Maybe builders put in Korean galvanized pipe. Wonderful!

But along came complaints. My pipes are leaking. The Korean galvanized pipes, so widely used, did not consider sediment buildup and therefore leaked. This gave way to copper. Copper, itself, is very expensive. Pound for pound, almost as much as a diamond. Don't know why since this country has an abundance of copper. Oh well!

There are two types of copper approved by most building departments. Type M and Type L. Type M is a thinner wall and is not suggested unless you are looking for cost savings. Type L is a thicker copper and will hold up as long as you own your home. They won't leak unless they are not properly sealed at the joints and joints are not cleaned properly. Soldering copper pipes is a job for an experienced professional. First timers rarely can do this job properly.

The innovation of ABS was first used around 1960. Today's ABS pipes are the best rain and sewer lines you can want since there is no possibility of root infestation and there is not the possibility of gunk deposits. If your house sits for a long period during construction or for any other reason, gunk will collect in pipes. But if you have ABS, a rooter will clean it out very easily without damage to the pipe walls.

ABS is the best option available today.

EXTERIOR

Various Stucco Finishes

Drive down your street and most likely you will see different color pallets on each house. Does this mean all is good? No, not at all. Some will appeal to one and some to others but, and it is a big but, would it appeal to a potential buyer?

The answer is the color applied to the right places and the colors used.

First, let's preface that white and black are not colors. With that said, paint your cabinets and ceilings white. Outstanding!

Start with the front of your house (first impression), colors would be white or gray. Exception, when homeowner's associations demand their color coordination or a majority of homes have a certain neighborhood look. Consider a black front door. Not for you? Then don't do it.

Paint all trim white. This includes fascia, mouldings, around windows, windows, and siding (unless the whole house is siding, then paint it gray).

Why? More than 85% of homeowners want this look.

Blue-gray is rapidly becoming the color of choice. These are paint colors that increase market value.

INTERIOR

Don't Be Misguided

Gray can be your color of choice for your interior. Gray was popular during the mid-century era, but then earth tones, such as brown and tan emerged. This author's house is of the earth tone pallet. To each his own! But gray has emerged today with many shades to satisfy you. There is cool gray with lots of blue/gray. There is warm gray with lots of yellow. Whichever you choose, don't mix.

Visit the building center or paint store and put together a pallet either cool or warm. Use your choice for the walls and cabinets only. You can choose three colors: one for the main part of the house, one for bedrooms, and one for smaller areas, such as the power room.

Everything else to be painted white. White mouldings, white doors and trim, and white ceilings. Remember, this author is *all knowing*. Resale, resale, resale! Keep in mind, you want to color up and not color down. Color up means appealing to the average buyer.

Many designers and homeowners think, wrongfully, that putting various colors in the rooms are attractive. Attractive to whom? Don't be misguided. Don't paint rooms various colors. Use only gray or earth tones if you wish, but stay to a pallet.

Pink, you might think, is good for a girl's bedroom but it will not fit. Don't do it. Period. Your young son will plead for chartreuse color walls. But hold steadfast. Don't do it. He will be happy in his new room without the chartreuse walls. If he wants chartreuse, then give him a chartreuse painted mirror frame.

So you don't want to add on, tear down walls, or do anything that requires a permit. This is called "cosmetic remodeling." You just want to spruce up your house for a quick sale or to move out and rent it to someone. Paint is not expensive. You may think a buyer can repaint the wall after they move in but you want to create a first impression.

The number one item to confront is painting. Here is where the homeowner in a semi-panic stage goes wrong. They paint everything white thinking white looks clean and will appeal to the buyer or renter. Not so. (FYI: The paint roller has only been around since 1940 when Canadian Norman Bakkey brought it to the market.)

1. Choose three or four family of colors (three for smaller house or four for a larger house).
2. The walls of each interior room to be any of these colors. You can use gloss, semi-gloss, low sheen or eggshell finish.
3. The exterior walls to be any one of these colors.
4. Interior and exterior trim to be gloss white. Use white vinyl windows.
5. Front door can be one of these colors or another from the same family of colors, or natural wood-stained.
6. Ceilings to be low sheen (flat) white. Period!
7. Carpet, hardwood and tile to be from the same family of colors.

As an example, let's say you choose gray. If you have an average size house, then choose three shades or variations of gray. Visit the home center and ask to be helped choosing three gray colors in the same family, such as: gray blue as compared to gray yellow or gray red.

Additionally, you want your choices to be either warm gray or cool gray but not mixed. You may have to do research to get it right.

Now you have three shades of gray. Paint the kitchen and adjoining rooms one color. Paint the master bedroom and master bath another. Paint all other walls the third color. All ceilings to be white. All woodwork to be white. Cabinets to be white, an island can be gray. Anything not part of the gray walls to be white. That goes also for the exterior.

You have something different in mind? Then prepare to cry when the house does not sell for the asking price or when renters take too long to decide. Make sure you have plenty of towels.

Replacing windows, if you can afford it, adds a great resale value. Use double pane windows for energy efficiency. Windows facing the front of the house should have grids and all the rest should be plain glass. No exceptions. Period!

After windows are the hardwood floors. No question. Use composite non-scratch flooring. The renters don't care but the buyers sure do. Besides this type of flooring will last fifty years showing only minimum wear. If you are fifty years old, stick around and see for yourself.

AESTHETICS

Brighten your life

Houses three centuries ago in Europe had flooring that only lasted a small period of time. The flooring does not come close to today's composite. You be the judge and jury.

Remodeling the kitchen or bathrooms does not come under the cosmetic column. If you do the other three things: painting, windows and floors, then remodeling the kitchen and bath may be a cost you do not want to pay for at this time.

You want to sell your house after doing the cosmetics and not remodeling the kitchen and bath? Good, as long as you get your asking price. Case closed.

ENERGY SAVINGS

Invest in the Future

Not everyone buys into energy savings. Certainly not the homeless, not homeowners living in the rain forest, not many living in Hawaii, Puerto Rico, and not the upper class.

But wait. Most of the upper class do care about energy savings. They install as much energy saving of these items as they can. For two reasons. First, the departments require they do so and they want to be part of the "Save the Planet" syndrome.

Energy is of only two aspects: one is water and the other is electricity. You may live in a beach home but you cannot use ocean water. Every house in America must have clean water piped to them. The less water you use means more for your neighbors. Aforementioned in other segments of this book, water consumption can be controlled.

You have to do your part. In arid portions of this country, it is essential to share water with everyone. But even if you live in Louisiana, the water must be purified in order to use it. This is not an inexpensive procedure. There may be lots of water outside but you need purified water to drink.

When Columbus discovered America, the word America came from an Italian in 1506. His name was America Geshepe. He said, "Let's name this land after me."

At this time, only 22% of this country was covered in greenery. Today, it is up to 62%. This includes your front yard.

How did this triple in these years? The botanists of America. They do not get the credit they deserve. The botanists came up with a solution for falling trees for construction use. They presented a replanting system that today is a marvel. More trees are planted in America than are cut down for use in construction. These are unsung heroes, to say the least. If you stay at Caesars Palace in Las Vegas, in the original towers built fifty years ago, you will have a lot of water coming out of the shower head. When Caesars Palace remodeled their older towers, they installed showers that have a restriction device allowing less water. These are much like your shower heads at home.

Why restrict water in Las Vegas? Water comes from Lake Mead and the lake is huge. But Las Vegas is not selfish. They know that this water is also used by millions of homeowners south, down the line.

There's a restriction built into every shower head available today in this country. When you take a shower, think of Las Vegas' selflessness. Remember that a shower takes less water than a bath tub only half full. That is the main reason showers should be built in every bathroom.

The biggest use of water is in your landscape. Know what time of day to water in order to give the best possible absorption for your plants to water properly. Most people feel they should water when the sun goes down. Wrong. Watering from 4 a.m. to 4 p.m. is best for your landscape. The majority feel that watering when the sun is out causes the water to evaporate. Not true. The sun will not penetrate into the soil more than a fraction. If you plant a lawn and only water at night, if will grow slowly. Guaranteed.

Electricity has been a major luxury for decades. The less we consume, the lower the cost. But this is not necessarily so. Every municipality has an electric division. They charge an exorbitant amount for electricity to your home. Much more than is necessary.

The problem is, these divisions have a very highly-paid staff. They need money and lots of it!

In our lifetime, we have known electricity to be a way of life. Less than 150 years ago there were no electrical appliances and only a few wall outlets. Today we have convention ovens, forced air systems for air conditioning, and plug-in outlets for electric cars. With all these innovations, we are asked to save and cut back. Energy saving is being addressed on two fronts. You must do whatever you can to conserve water and electricity, all the while using the air conditioning system.

If you live in a remote part of this country, then you create your own energy. And the rest of us could learn from you.

The research and development (R&D) staff in manufacturing companies are working full time to better address the energy items we use. They call this "investing in the future."

When it comes to energy savings, the future is here. Compare one century ago to today. Half a century ago, insulation was good. Today insulation is much more efficient. Today insulation is required in walls, ceilings and floors.

One century ago, we had single-pane glass dating back to ancient China. Today, only double-pane glass is required, and in some cases, as designed by energy engineers, triple glass is required. Along with double-pane glass doors and windows came safety glass which prevents intruders from entering. Additionally, tempered glass is available, which is the same as automobile glass.

A huge energy-efficient requirement not known by the average homeowner is the radiant barrier. This is a coated plywood sheathing applied to the roof during framing. The radiant barrier reflects heat away from the structure. When radiant barrier plywood is installed during the framing stage, you can stand in the house even before the walls are up and feel twenty degrees cooler than the outside temperature.

Appliance manufacturers are improving energy efficiency. These include meter box, washer and dryer, hood, dishwasher, range and microwaves. Some are more energy efficient than others.

Aforementioned, LED is a huge energy savings. You want nothing other than LED interior and exterior lighting. LED is relatively new but it hit the scene with a blast. Maximize effectiveness, the future is here!

KNOW YOUR PRODUCT

Life-Changing Experience

When shopping at the food mart, you have a preconceived idea of what you are shopping for. Once there, you check out prices of fruits and vegetables and compare the prices mentally to what they cost before. You may skip the strawberries since they are very high priced (out of season) and go for the bananas. As you proceed around the store, there is a good chance you will see something new. For example, applesauce with a spicy favor. This may not appeal to you, but you take note. You have become very familiar with this store. You know basically every aisle, every shelf, and the items on the shelf. This comes with multiple visits, of course.

How does this relate to your project? The store is your project. The aisle is your plan. The cabinets, tile, and stone are the shelves, and the items on the shelves are your details, i.e. plumbing fixtures, appliances, and roofing.

You can't do enough research. If you start in January, by July new items will appear. This author installed a pocket door. This is the same door that has been around for a century but now has an improved track for the rollers. Then along came the self-closing pocket door. It would have worked well but…too late. The door is already installed. Research!

How many trips will you make to meet your architect or to the building departments? Don't count them. There will be many.

You have limited time due to miscellaneous restraints. You must put your available time to the best use. You cannot do enough research. Research everything from appliances to roofing. You may be limited to the size of appliances but not roofing. Don't leave the roofing choice to the architect. Research it yourself.

What is your preferred façade (the face of the building)? Stone, stucco, siding, or brick? Research. This work is called "down time." When you have given the architect your desired plan, take the time to research more and give any updates to the architect at your next meeting. The more you research, the closer you will get to the ideal finished project that you will be happy with.

Ask to speak to the chief architect—and the same for the contractor. Request personal attention. You will be pleasantly surprised when you present to them what you have researched. Ask for opinions and suggestions. Become a team player. Act with aplomb!

FIRE PREVENTION

Destroying Everything Combustible

When houses were made of wood with thatched roofs constructed of palm fronds or straw, they burned in a flash and were difficult to extinguish with buckets of water. A tragedy for sure, but in only a few weeks, a new wooden house was constructed in its place. You don't have this luxury.

Unfortunately, in two centuries, we have not come a long way in fire prevention. The Babylonians' stone houses were fireproof, but since the roof was made of wood, it burned and collapsed into the house destroying everything combustible. Their answer was to install a solid timber roof, which was more effective, but very costly. Even *it* did not hold up in a major area fire.

The Roman emperor Nero watched Rome burn in 64 AD—not just a few houses, but the majority of the city. Nero blamed the fire on the Christians but the Romans were among the first city planners. The senators spent many hours debating the proper layout of their cities and requirements of the building to be fire resistant. This formed the first world's planning department. The Roman Empire was huge but it fell to the activists. No more wars, no more spreading the ownership of lands and no more conquering. Stop and think what would have been the makeup of the globe if the Romans continued on.

Europe would have been under Roman rule. They would have sailed to the far seas with no restrictions. America could have been part of the Roman Empire. But isn't America a glance of Roman system of government? We have the senate with senators to govern. We have building departments to regulate what is safe to build.

Most of all, our citizens are much like the Romans enjoying the fruits of the government requirements. But with restrictions, the people did not readily accept their new rules until their house withstood a fire. Back to fire prevention.

Notice the author does not use the term "fire proof." Little, if anything, is fire proof. A bulletproof vest is bulletproof until a 250-caliber bullet hits it and penetrates. So let's stay with fire prevention.

With that said, houses today are nearing fireproof but are not there yet. You may not care if your house will burn down because you have fire insurance. Fire insurance is required on all loan mortgages. You cannot get a loan on your house unless you have, among other requirements, fire insurance. This insurance fee is a delight with underwriters since so few homes burn.

This author lives two blocks from a fire station. An interview with the fire chief culminated in the words "We serve 4,000 homes and only seven, in an average year, have fire damage. We stand ready for a catastrophe at all times."

Out of every one million homes, only fifty-five burn down each year. This figure has increased since in many areas, such as California, 500 homes were recently destroyed in thirty days. This leaves 2,249, 000 homes not affected by fire in the state. But all have to pay fire insurance premiums in the country. A fire insurance company has never gone out of business due to paying out for damages.

What can you do? You can reduce your premium. If you have a more fire-resistant house, the insurance by underwriters will be less. Remember the insurance agent you use does not have final say; it's the underwriter. There are about sixteen underwriters in this country backing the premiums of agents with federal loans and direct aid for natural disasters.

Now to your house and what you can do to keep it safe from fire and keep your premiums low. The first is having a good roof. You probably don't have straw. The department rates "Class A" roofing as those that will withstand sparks from ashes which will simmer and die when landing within one hour.

If you have a wood shingle roof, which is now outlawed in most of this country, the embers will find a home and burn the house down. The minimum "Class A" roof is a composition roofing supplied by thirty-two manufacturers. Composition roofing is far from fireproof but is the minimum requirement since it's the least expensive.

As you see new developments springing up, you will notice concrete tile roofing. This material is a huge expense for developers, but with discriminating home buyers such as you, this is a must for fire prevention—also, it looks beautiful.

Concrete tile is made of two forms: the flat tile, which is preferred for contemporary and traditional homes, and the tops and pans, also called "S" tile. Research. These tiles are commonly used in Mediterranean and Spanish design. These roofs will not burn; flying embers do not affect them. If a burning tree falls on these roofs, it will not burn through. The tree will burn out.

There is still the issue of vents. Vents will allow embers to penetrate into your attic and start a fire not easily extinguishable. Vents are a necessity for attic ventilation unless you have a flat roof. It is a fact that modern flat roofed homes are the least fire damaged. The downside is that there is no attic, no crawl space and no good place to put pipes and ducts. The trade-off is the beauty of the contemporary home. Arizona, here we come!

In the event that you want a contemporary house with a flat roof, a crawl space can be designed between the ceiling joists and the roof rafters with attic space and vents. For years, vents required 1/4" spacing but 1/8" spacing is more fire resistant. It's called 1/8" mesh.

So you have tiled roofing, 1/8" mesh and still your house burns down? Devastating. What could have caused this? Answer: the eves. If embers or a tree on fire hits your house, flames will find a path of least resistance: the wooden eves.

Have you noticed if you leave a donut out on the patio overnight it will attract ants? How do ants know it's there? Somehow they do and you know the next time not to leave inviting foods out. Same holds true to the organic embers. They find the way to continue the burning process—as if they have a life of their own.

Eves support the projection of the roof where the roof extends past the exterior of the house to keep the rain water from washing against the walls. For a millennium, the eves were made of wood. Wood burns. Duh!

Your eves need to be as fire resistant as your roof and walls. Stucco on the eves is the most popular solution but this does not work with every home style. Use what the department calls a one-hour protection, which is a thin (2") wood material (2" x 6" T&G will suffice).

Depending on your architectural style, eliminate eves and your problem is solved. But is it what you want? Work on it!

Roofing, covered. Now what about the exterior walls? Stucco was first introduced to California in 1885. In the beginning, cement was adhered to the walls, which was a takeoff from the Aztecs who put clay on the exterior walls to prevent heat intrusion. (There was no thought to fire prevention at the time.)

During the same period, England used a clay composite to cover the exterior walls. This was made of clay and straw. Again, there was no thought to fire prevention. The objective was only cosmetic.

During approximately the 5th Century, England and France began building houses with brick. Again, not for fire prevention but for cosmetic reasons. England and France had not had a major fire catastrophe so the brick houses were not tested.

But this country did. In 1925, San Francisco houses were not built with brick or cement. They were built with wood siding. A major fire tore through the city and was devastating. Most of the city burned to the ground. In 1926, San Francisco rebuilt 20,000 homes in one year.

Before the fire, San Francisco homes, like many middle-class homes in this country, had wood siding made from either Douglas fir or redwood. Wood roofs and wood siding would burn to the ground quickly. The fire department responded with trucks and hand-held, two-man pump that pumped water into the flames.

Today, stucco is used on 90% of middle class homes. Together with concrete tire roofing and stucco walls, the American home became more fireproof and therefore, most valuable. Needless to say, stone and brick are fire resistant with brick veneer becoming used more for aesthetics.

Homeowners in America did not take heed of the fact that siding burns rapidly. From the beginning wood siding was the preference of home builders due to the look they wanted. Cement siding is available today. It looks similar to the wood but will not burn. Now you have a choice: stucco or cement siding. Good options.

To note, stucco is not the application by itself. Stucco is the finish 1/8" coat applied after the cement has cured for five days. Stucco comes with a cement additive, dry, ready to mix with water. This cement base stucco takes twenty-eight days to harden fully. Acrylic stucco, premixed and ready to apply, dries as fast as paint. Neither requires painting.

Then along came drywall in 1956 in America. First, ½", which lasted only twenty years. In 1976, 5/8" thick Type X drywall came on the market and it was a huge hit, since it was also fire resistant. Then, drywall was only used on garage walls adjoining the house and under stairwells but today it is used everywhere interior walls are finished.

Then along came the dreaded sprinklers. These have been the bane of homeowners ever since it was first enacted by the city "know it alls." Sure, it will put out or diminish a fire but it also causes more water damage than the fire itself.

This author was playing poker in Las Vegas across the street from the old MGM Hotel when it caught fire. Patrons were yelling, "The hotel is on fire." Our table casually finished the game and gathered up our chips before leaving. This author walked across the street to see people jumping out of windows and some were very high. What a spectacle! Following this catastrophe, all hotels were required to have sprinklers and existing hotel rooms had to be retrofitted with both alarms and sprinklers.

When the Vegas Monte Carlo caught fire, the sprinklers did the job very well to save lives. But this isn't the case for residential sprinkler systems. They will go off even when there is too much smoke from the kitchen, leading to untold water damage.

Let's review: You want cement tile roof, stucco or stone veneer, cement siding, Type X drywall, fireproof vents, fireproof eves (elsewhere in this book) and trees not planted near the house. There is no need for sprinklers. Period! This should keep you well rested at night. Brick is sustainable.

Bottom line: If your neighbor's house catches fire then yours will be left standing and intact. You will have bragging rights. This is the present and future home in America. Fire prevention by systematic logging.

Catastrophic fire can't be eliminated but the devastation can be drastically reduced with water reservoirs and ground clearance. Five decades ago, we had fire breaks, which were dirt roads out from wherever there was a potential for brush fire. These dirt roads are gone and fire has ravaged for years, killing people.

Fire Extinguishers

Fire extinguishers save lives and property. Every residential house, whether supplied with smoke alarms and/or water sprinkler systems, must have one or more extinguishers. Experts recommend one unit for every 600 square feet of living space plus one in the garage.

Extinguishers fight oil, gasoline, flammable liquids, electrical, wood, paper and cloth fires. Mount one on the wall or leave it freestanding in your garage, kitchen, bedroom closet, living room, hall and basement.

To use, simply pull the safety pin (easily removed) and aim at the fire swiping side to side.

Check your unit, periodically, to observe if the gauge is in the white section. If it is, you should replace it.

Home centers sell twin value packs for about $30. This is a good preventative investment. Only use ABC rated units.

Note: This author had a unit for fifteen years thinking it's okay to use when needed, but it does not work. Follow the instructions. Bottom line: the unit lasts a long time but it should be replaced after six years. Do not pull the pin until ready to use (do not test). Once the trigger is pulled it will shut down and need to be replaced.

TAKE THE TIME (Maybe Find A...)

Believing in Your Project

The key to the successful culmination of your project is directly related to the time you put into it. My son's pappy said, "Haste makes waste."

Drive 100 mph to the grocery store to get one quart of milk. Get into a major accident and wind up in the hospital. Your mother or spouse comes to visit you and says, "When you left the house you forgot your wallet to pay for the milk."

Slow down. We don't have all the time in the world, but we do have current time. This is the time you have to compile research for an ideal house. It may not be perfect but you can always say you gave it your 100% effort.

Start with a binder (you may need more than one). Categorize everything from appliance information to pictures you have taken. (Take many.)

Take time with your architect. This may mean additional costs but it will be worth it in the end. Take time to visit the building departments. Don't leave a single stone unturned. Ask a million questions. You will get a million answers. You will be surprised at how helpful they will be.

Take time with your contractor. Most homeowners feel they are so busy with their daily lives, they don't have time. Discuss every detail. Budget your time during this process. It's a tremendous investment and endeavor.

Unfortunately, you cannot buy a finished product the way you want it with a stroke of the pen. If you don't want to go through this time-consuming process, sell your house, move up to a bigger and better one and pay the huge property tax.

Big downside, taxes! The increase in property taxes on a remodel is much lower than buying a new house and paying the sale price tax. When building new, it's the same. The property tax on a new house you build is always less than purchasing another.

Over ten years, you will save the majority of your costs in taxes if you build. When your house is sold for a fixed amount, the new buyer must pay the full tax amount. Let's return to taking the time.

You must invest one day per week—it could be Saturday, to compile your portfolio. It does not have to be all day Saturday, but this is the day you may have most available and the home supply companies are open, although some may close as early as 1 p.m.. You should also research items online. Note items you want to discuss with the architect.

The architect will take your project just so far. This author summarizes only about 80%; the other 20% is up to you to decide, such as appliances, stone, tile, and plumbing fixtures.

There is no need to burden the architect with cabinet details. You know what you want. With this said, you can instead request the architect do an all-inclusive plan. This is costly but relieves you of any time and decision making. If you have the bucks, then this is a way to go for believing in the architect to present you with your dream project.

As you have read this book, you have learned the pros and cons of doing your own research. There are two ways to complete a project: putting in the time versus paying an architect. When the job is done, you have to live with it—the same as buying a completed house.

Or, you can end up with a project that has your blood and sweat into it by taking lots of time. In the end, you can say, "I did it my way." Take the time and be timely.

AMENITIES: KITCHEN

- Soap dispensers at main sink, new are top-loading, no need to go under sink to refill.
- Second dishwasher with drawers for light cleaning.
- Cutlery drawer.
- Touch or push-open drawers and doors.
- Soft-closing drawers and doors.
- Spice cabinet. Pull out; not next to range unless appliance sides are insulated.
- Volume control of speakers to family room TV with space behind to put communication box.
- Wall TV with ceiling speakers.
- Security screen to monitor front and rear of house.
- Heated floors at main sink area only or use cork mat or cork flooring.
- Lighting switches where you can turn on a ceiling light in three different locations.
- Island outlets at both ends (also ceiling light switches from the island).
- Under cabinet lighting for ambience, also kills bacteria. Install a dimmer.
- Pantry with non-stick shelves (melamine).
- Pantry with auto light (no switch) when door is opened and light comes on with motion.
- Glass doors to pantry that says "pantry" etched in glass.
- Glass cabinet doors with lighting and glass shelves.
- Storage in back of second island with doors only (should be only 12" deep).

- Dishwasher with recess handle so as to not catch clothing, adjustable sliding drawers, convert hard water to soft water and light under unit to show when turned on.
- Instant hot water, also cold-filtered (unit under sink).
- Refrigerator with build-in filter if you have water in the door.
- Bun warmer, a.k.a. a "warming drawer" (also good to warm towels prior to going into pool on a cooler day).
- Colored stainless steel appliances with finger/print resistance.
- Smaller vegetable sink in island on a counter neared the refrigerator. Allow 18" minimum each side for food preparation.
- Butler's pantry. Research. See Kitchen section.
- Recycling double baskets attached to cabinet front.
- Appliance garage if you have the space.
- Air switch to turn on disposer. No electricity. Safe. Not easy for children to turn on.
- Wine refrigerator, a.k.a. wine cooler. Comes counter or full height, 15" – 24" wide.
- Drawer microwave. Good for short people.
- Drawer refrigerator. Good access for kids (two drawers).

AMENITIES: BATH

- Foot massage about six inches above floor wall of seat. This will require another diverter. Plan ahead.
- Chandelier in center master bath or bladed fan.
- Handheld shower head. This is adjustable and can be used for combination handheld and shower head also used for smaller showers.
- Body sprays. Three on one side and two more on opposing side (works best if not more than five inches apart).
- Handicap shower without a dam. Wheelchair/handicap. Must be framed properly.
- Small mosaic tile shower floor one inch by one inch to keep from slipping (comes in glass and porcelain tile made by all tile manufacturers), also two by two inch works well.
- Spa tub with both water and air jets.
- Tub valve one side of tub to control spout from ceiling made by Kohler. Research.
- Vanity counter with 3-inch drawer (could be same height as other counters about 34 inches from floor).
- Wall sconces each side of mirror.
- Small pendant light, center of mirror, ten inches from wall, and 84 inches from floor (wall sconces and pendant lights controller with one switch).
- Shower floor drain to one side. Research.
- Digital shower with no knobs or handles, simply control by pushing buttons.
- Shower seat with warmer stone.
- Shower doors frameless and self-cleaning. Research.

AMENITIES: OTHER ROOMS

- Crown moulding in all rooms, can be either streamline or detailed.
- Exterior doors with louvers between the two panes of glass. Adjustable with levers.
- Exterior doors with shatterproof glass (burglar proof).
- Laundry with front-loading washer and dryer, saves energy.
- Put a fogger to kill insects in attic every three to six months. Research.
- Ductless A/C wall unit (invented in Japan in 1970 with remote controls). Good for attic, basement or garage.
- Radiant barrier plywood to repeal heat into attic. Research.
- Gas-driven generator when there is a power outage. Research.
- Construction paint to paint on the floors where you intend to put cabinets and furniture. This will line up with your overhead lighting.
- Build in a wall and/or floor safe.

5

Know the Unknowns

Know the Unknowns

FENG SHUI

Timeless

The term Feng Shui translates to "wind water" in English. Feng Shui is a traditional Chinese practice that binds the universe, earth, and humanity together. You are only concerned with how it pertains to your home.

You may embrace Feng Shui or you may not. This author suggests: Don't take a chance and do your house Feng Shui proper. It's not a burden; it's for better living.

There are two directions to go with Feng Shui. The one used by Chinese teachers is complicated and does not fit well with American homes. You should not care about what is required for a window placement; you care about the view. You should not care which corner of the room faces which direction. Feng Shui is an ancient belief that every square foot of your house makes for better living. This is commendable but does not fit all that well with today's Feng Shui lifestyle.

This author's observation is if a room is placed to be Feng Shui proper and does not take advantage of the view or watching over the children at play, then it is archaic and should be visited with pragmatism.

The Feng Shui direction to go is the modern version. A modern Feng Shui teacher could look at your plans and make suggestions. The teacher can also walk through your house and suggest remodeling that will be Feng Shui proper. This is a suggested investment.

This author believes adhering to the basics is what will make your house special. There are major and minor suggestions. This major items are: No mirrors in bedrooms; when entering the front door you should not see through to the rear yard (this is called bad Chi. You don't want bad Chi).

Bottom line, Feng Shui basics definitely add value to your house. Do what is basic. Don't take a chance. Feng Shui adds value, never diminishes it. Prior to 2000, Koreans would not accept Feng Shui, but now all Asians, after being privy to their values, are considering adapting Feng Shui to their floor plan. You could say Feng Shui or you could say good planning. Both are correct.

The foot of the stairs should not face the entry door. Doors to rooms on the opposite side of the hall should not be in line. The kitchen sink must face the rear yard whether it is on a wall or on the island.

Never have the kitchen sink face the limited side yard. Toilets should never be visible from the adjacent rooms, such as halls or bedrooms, when the bathroom door is open.

- Mirror in bathrooms, preferable full height, such as on a door.
- No mirrors in bedrooms.
- The bed is not to face the entry door of the bedroom nor directly into the bathroom. (A major Feng Shui item.)
- No open space for insects to inhabit. Get a grasp on this. You will feel the difference.

- Never put vaulted gable ceilings in a sleeping area. It may lead you soon to be under the knife.
- Make your landscape Feng Shui proper. Put in a small wind turbine or metal wind chimes, a fire pit or fireplace, running waterfall or a fountain, at least one major tree, and keep your yard weed free.
- A growing population is embracing Feng Shui. Be ready. You love your house; your house will love you.

SAFETY AND SECURITY

Be Alarmed

It goes without saying, you want to be safe and secure and free from pests.

In the Middle Ages, homes were built so close to each other that they had little privacy and were not safe and secure. Back then, as soon as you rid your house of rodents, the neighbors' rodents would find their way in. (See segment on Pests.)

Doors and windows were easily broken into. The only security was a gun. From the time of Jesus to the time of Napoleon, life was not sacred. There was a movie made called *Zulu*. The British were positioned to hold out until help arrived. The invaders sent warriors to attack and many died in the advance. The chief said he was allowing the warriors to die in order to count the guns.

How much is your life worth? This author's mother once said that every child is worth a million dollars. How much are you worth now?

Okay, let's say you have three children. That's three million dollars. You need to do everything possible to protect this investment. Sure, you can't set a dollar amount on your children but you can give them the best safety and security money can buy.

Let's address the last subject first: rodents. A roofer once told this author that every house has them. Knowing this, you must know what to do. This author thought long and hard about inserting the rat situation in this book. But how can one write a complete book without covering the unmentionable?

If you have a tight enclosed house where no rats can find their way in, but you leave the house vacant for three or four months, you will attract rats. They can find their way in spaces you thought impossible. Accept this, since you cannot find every small hole and if you do, they will come down the chimney. Santa Claus hates rats!

Let's look at the sequence. From the time you start remodeling to the finish, rodents will not appear. Guaranteed. They will not stay in any construction zone. It's the noise! But now you've finished with construction. Poison in the attic is a must from day one. Put a tray of rat poison in the attic and under the house (this will poison neighbor's cats, raccoons, possums, and anything else that takes the bait) with a pile of poison. Check it once a month. If the poison is gone, it does not mean rats are got. Add more poison.

Due to government regulations on poisons, of which we are thankful, poisons are very costly. However, know that this is a trade-off. You may be putting other animals at risk. Make sure that the area under your house and in the attic is inaccessible for any animals due to the fact that they could be poisoned.

If you do nothing about rats, they will eat away at your electrical system, which will compromise your safety. Have an inspector, after completion, go into the attic to see what daylight is visible from the attic to the outside. This light is a rat entrance.

Bigger than rats are the burglars. They don't want to eat wires; they want to steal from you. There are two types of burglars: the professional and the neighborhood kids. If you leave your house vacant for a long time, say two weeks or longer, this raises a flag.

Generally, the neighborhood kids will not steal much. Most likely, electronic equipment or alcoholic drinks. But the professional thief will ransack your bedroom looking for jewelry, cash, electronic items and fire arms. The neighborhood thief will do little damage to your home while the professional thief will do whatever it takes to sort through available items to steal.

Law enforcement, say those living on busy streets, have a greater percentage of home break-ins. This is obvious: The thief has an easy get-away.

Okay, you can position a machine gun at the front door and one at the back door. What you really need to do is in keeping with what is requirement by the departments.

First, you already have in your new or remodeled house, double-pane glass in doors and windows that is strong and difficult to shatter by the burglar. It is loud to shatter and is not easily done. You need to add a camera at the front door linked to an app in your Smart Phone. The objective is to deter the burglar in any way you can. Go to a security company and purchase signs that read "Security by Apex" or whoever. Put these signs on your landscape in both the front and backyard (as this is the entrance most thieves will come in through).

The burglar does not know if they are real but they will not take a chance. Better yet, an alarm system for all doors and windows. If you are away for long periods then get openings alarmed. Burglars hate the alarm noise.

There is another way. Use a security monitoring company. Little girl to mother, "Daddy said there's no such thing as a boogeyman. Why do we need a burglar alarm?"

Locking the gates to the rear yard is a deterrent. The best lock would be a key or a digital opening lock. You can have it open during every day and locked when you are away. Do not use padlocks since they can be easily cut (and you might not remember where you hid the key!).

A personal safe is a "must" in every home. You have the luxury. Build-in a safe or two. A floor safe is the best for smaller items, such as documents and money. Also, a built-in wall safe. When your safe is built-in, it is virtually impossible to remove. Guns must be stored safely. Period!

Let's go back to the machine gun. Have you seen the placard in front of a house that says "Protected by (and a drawing of a gun)." Law enforcement says this is the very best deterrent against intruders. Not for everyone but the bottom line is safety for everyone.

Of course, the new alarm system will put the dog out of business.

MAKE YOUR HOUSE LOOK NEW

Flying off the Market

Add a smaller room addition, then you may want to stop there. If you have a two bedroom house and add one more bedroom and bath, then you may want to stop there. If you are remodeling a kitchen and a bath, then you may want to stop there. When you're remodeling 25% or less of your house, then you may want to stop there.

But if you have a larger project of more than 25% of your house, you should spruce up the balance. A majority of home-owners remodeling usually only paint the balance of the interior. But this is the time to upgrade the balance of doors and mouldings and if the walls and ceilings need smoothing, then do that also. And a good time to upgrade some electrical including the main panel. Oh, and don't forget the windows and fireplace surround.

If your budget allows, replace the floors with new engineered wood throughout. Lastly, paint. This will make your entire house look new and it's an amazing feeling of satisfaction. You may only remodel once and once is enough.

With that said, the best increase in your home's value is an addition since it adds footage and the overall look to your house, both interior and exterior.

There are other, unending items you can add to your house to make it look like a new house that will compete with a newly constructed house. One such item is lighting. Install only 27K recess lights, but do not put in too many. If you do, add a dimmer. Recess lights can be installed in the ceiling without breaking the plaster by using retrofit units. There will be small holes where the electrician has to fish lines to the switches. Patch and paint.

Mouldings need replacing. Put a new sample moulding next to your existing one. If many coats of paint has changed the configuration so it looks worn, then replace with new. Today, we use water-based paint but older coats of thick oil-based paint makes the moulding look beaten.

There are three types of mouldings in your house. The baseboard at the floor, the casing, which goes around the doors and window openings, and crown mouldings at the ceiling. (The word molding is British for moulding.) Moulding manufacturers in America use the spelling "moulding."

When installing wood flooring, it is necessary to leave a gap of 3/8" against walls for expansion. This means the base moulding must be more than ¾" thick or additional moulding must be used. This is called a "base shoe."

The base shoe was used for centuries even when the base board of ¾" thickness covered the expansion gap. But back then, there was a secondary reason to use the base shoe—to cover the gap between the baseboard and the flooring not allowing insects to hide. This is true since the flooring was uneven and left gaps as wide as ¼".

But today's flooring is not as wavy. Engineered flooring can be laid without base shoe but will need a small amount of caulking. Use only paint-grade base board where the paintable caulking will blend in.

Most likely, you have mouldings around your doors and windows (unless you have a contemporary house where no mouldings are used). Contemporary homes make up less than 5% of American homes. That doesn't mean contemporary homes are a small amount and the future will bring more. The future will be traditional exterior with contemporary interiors.

As for your house with mouldings around your doors and windows: the doors are always the same. Windows can be picture-frames (same moulding used on all four sides) or with a window sill and a corresponding moulding under called a "skirt". Skirts are generally used in classic homes or those built prior to 1940.

Crown moulding was first introduced in parts of Europe around 500 AD. The purpose then was to cover up for the plasterers who did not even the corners. The crown was made of plaster and only used in upper class homes. Wood crown was introduced in this country around 1750 (the era of 1750 was the beginning of architectural revolution in this country). This was when the Americans didn't care what was going on in the world; they wanted what they wanted. This has held true all over the country.

The north built city homes, the south built plantations. The plantations were large but they both had something in common—crown moulding. Crown moulding back then was boring. It had very little detail and was small in size.

Unless you have a contemporary house without mouldings, the crown moulding is for you. You don't need more than a 6" crown, since a larger moulding will be overbearing. Larger rooms, larger crown moulding. When you put crown in your existing rooms, it will enhance the beauty and add resale value. A good thing.

This author suggests you use the same crown moulding throughout your house. Put it in all rooms except closets, stairs leading to the attic, and garages.

Window replacement. You don't want anyone to walk through your house and see your improvements and the old windows. Change to vinyl. More than 80% of homeowners approve of vinyl windows. If a buyer walks through your house and sees all windows are vinyl, they know the windows will not only last but they will be easily operable. If your budget warrants, change out to vinyl. It's called "retrofit".

Be a discriminating homeowner and you will appeal to the discriminating home buyer. Get top dollar.

REMODEL VS. REBUILD

Best of the Best

The author has designed this book to assist remodelers, but remodeling to achieve the end result might not be possible, so let's explore the possibility of tearing down the house and building a new structure.

This idea is a favorite for flippers who feel the best bang for the buck is to rebuild. Not always. Tearing down a house leaves you with land value. What is your lot worth without any structures? The biggest advantage is that you can build what you want. You can go from a one-story to a two-story or more.

There are a few factors to clarify the dilemma of remodeling versus rebuilding. First is the extent of remodeling. You may believe it is 50% of your house but it's really 60%, meaning, if you purchase a house for a given amount and tear is down, then you can recoup your investment by selling the vacant land. Does not seem logical. Then let's say your house is worth "X" dollars on your street. You will find a vacant lot on your same street will bring about the same price.

How can this happen? Investors and aggressive homeowners will pay top dollar for a vacant lot to build what they want. Location! And they can move faster to get building permits in most cases.

If your house burns down, naturally, you must rebuild. Follow the guidelines in this book to make your distraught life calmer. Your former house was a living space. Now make it into a jewel.

A big advantage is that the new house can become a two-story house with more rear yard. Everything is new. No need to keep the old lath and plaster and deteriorated siding.

Building a new house should follow all segments in this book to a T.

Now it's time to know exactly what to do. Follow the guidelines aforementioned and you will come up with a preliminary plan. Ask any good Realtor what the house will be worth when it is finished. Weigh this with your budget or your ability to finance.

Objective: Increase property value.

The vacant lot for sale will bring in the amount for which you purchased the house originally. Problem here, you are trading dollars. Not making business sense.

Now you have a vacant lot after the cost of the demolition and hauling. Next, you have architectural plans, engineering and permits to build the house of your dreams.

Most investors want to see a 20% return as a minimum. You can put together a good project by following this author to get a much better return on your investment. This is the Bible for home remodeling.

As the years pass, new building code requirements are legislated. Generally, when remodeling and adding to the existing structure, you do not have to comply with codes enacted after your house was built. If your existing house is too close to the property lines, then it may remain that way except the new addition will have to comply. Another big item is electrical. Whatever exists can remain but if you tear into the old portion of the house, then some—if not all—electrical will be required to be upgraded to conform to current codes. This can be a good thing if your budget warrants.

Weigh also the cost of making the existing part of the house look new, like the addition and other completely remodeled rooms.

You don't want the addition to look obvious. But with a master plan, you can do a majority of the work now and then refinance to do the balance at a later date. There is always time. So you are leaning toward tearing down your house and rebuilding using all the thought-out suggestions in this book. All those in favor raise your hand. Now you are committed.

The Advantages of a Tear-Down Versus a Rebuild

1. Do it your way. You have a choice where to put the garage and front door.
2. If your existing front setback is too deep and the ordinance allows you to build closer to the street, you can now have a larger rear yard.
3. Number one is you have the freedom to design as near a perfect house as possible. Time to reread this book. One option to explore, if you now have a one-story house, build a two-story.
4. A two-story house with an elevator will fetch top dollar.
5. When tearing down your house, get rid of shabby trees and shrubs and that old thick lawn that never looked evenly green.
6. Position your new house to take better advantage with views and sun shining in. Most houses can't be turned but it's possible to have the family room face north.
7. You will install all new pipes, ducts, drains, sewer lines and electrical that will last your lifetime.
8. In order to obtain financing, you may have to take out a second or third mortgage. If the total payments are 40%

of your monthly income, then go for it even if it means higher interest. About a year or more after you get final inspection, refinance all loans into one package at a lower interest rate.

9.   Roofing and roof structures are a significant factor in the longevity of your house. You may want a fireproof roof but your existing roof structure will not support heavy tiles. So when you rebuild, the engineer will factor in the roof structure.

Also, while at it, pay close attention to the pitch. The steeper the pitch, the longer lasting the roofing materials. A steeper roof may last fifty years. In Europe, tile roofs on heavy structures have held up for two or three centuries. No need to wait around that long. But they are fire-rated.

10. You may find more room for a pool house or guest house.

The Disadvantages of Tearing Down and Rebuilding

1.   Large amount of dollars for plans, engineering and department fees.

2.   If your front set back is too close, then you must comply with current set back requirements, generally, the average of the other homes on the street. This is called the prevailing set back.

3.   Everywhere in this country there are protected trees. If such a tree is close to your house then nothing will be said until you want to remove it. But now you can't rebuild as close as you were planning to. If you really want to build close to a protected tree, this author suggests you do. There are

options of getting department approval by either paying a substantial fee or having a botanist give you recommendations in writing.

4. Landscape and irrigation systems are a major expense. You want to stay physically fit? Do the planting yourself. If you stay physically fit, you can enjoy your house longer.

5. Irrigation is best left to the professionals. Okay, you want an automatic watering system? The digging and/or laying of pipes may be your calling. First, hire a consultant to help with the layout, or request the sprinkler company give you the option to do some work on it yourself.

6. Dumping fees and recycling fees could add up. The costs can be offset by selling as much of your discarded house as you can to collectors or donate to charitable organizations which is tax deductible.

7. The difficulty of obtaining financing or the money you need to do the complete project.

8. Determine what your payments on a newly consolidated mortgage will be when the time comes to refinance. Not everyone qualifies. You may qualify for a third mortgage but not a refinance. Look for a house in your neighborhood that closely resembles your house when finished, and get the current market value. Easy to do on the internet. Go to a bank and ask if you would pre-qualify. If yes, then proceed, but if not, determine how much would be available. This will tell you to rebuild or remodel.

You can still draw a master plan but only do what you can afford. If you can hold out until you or your spouse is sixty-two, then you can get a reverse mortgage. (More about that in another chapter.)

There is another way. The other way is for the entrepreneur in you to do 95% of what most homeowners will not attempt.

The flippers look for cosmetic fixes instead of good planning as outlined by this author. What would you rather have: a new hardwood floor or a kitchen with an island?

This leads to a story about Mrs. Fox who, after making desserts on the island noticed water gushing into the kitchen. Mr. Fox, not able to locate the water intrusion, went into the garage and retrieved a two-person rubber float. As they paddled around the kitchen they noticed a deserted island.

The sequence is simple. Get a house, remodel properly, taking as much time as it takes, sell and buy another and another. Become wealthy. It's the American capitalistic way.

Take as much time as it takes. All the while live in the houses so that you will have only one mortgage payment. After ten houses and twenty years, you will be living in a multimillion-dollar mortgage-free house, which only 8% of the population can afford.

The children will be inconvenienced but as they get older, they will be part of the plan because they will realize what the ultimate goal is and it will not be long before they will help you out. The children love to show the finished product to a prospective buyer. Oh, and there is a bottom line—it's called "inheritance."

HOMEOWNERS INSURANCE

House Can't be Carried Away

This author is not a big fan of insurance, collectively. Insurance companies are the largest in the world, they are regulated by the National Association of Insurance Commissioners (NAIC). They collect premiums and pay out claims. They all have one positive factor. They do pay out for damages and do it in a timely manner. If your house burns, they will pay you lots of money, even more than the replacement value, no questions asked.

But this author has a question. Why? The answer is the insurance companies have so much money they need to send it out. Why do they have all this money? The premiums they take in far exceed the payments that they make.

If you ask an executive of a major insurance company, "Why do you have so much money on hand?" they will always say they need to prepare for a catastrophe, such as the wildfires or floods. In 2017, the Tubbs Fire destroyed 5,000 homes and 2800 vehicles in California. All the insurance companies combined used only 16.5% of their reserves to pay out the claims. But one year later, they only paid 39% of the claims.

This is a good example of why only 5% of insurance companies filed bankruptcy or quit business in twenty-five years as compared to 22% of other corporations. This is a five to one ratio. Out of proportion!

You have homeowners' insurance, which you definitely want and need. Mortgage underwriters demand this of you. But the amount they charge is exorbitant. The underwriters base the insurance premium on the value of the house at the time of purchase. If your house burns down, the land does not burn and the foundation does not burn. So why pay insurance to replace the land and foundation? Be a fighter. Make sure the policy only covers replacement. Make the agent aware. Take a large deductible.

Now comes the further fight/argument. Have the architect design your house with fire-rated materials, such as stucco, cement siding, fire-retardant eve overhangs, proper ember preventing vents, a stone or brick veneer, fire-retardant roofing, such as concrete tile, trees not touching the house, wood fences not close to any structure, dual pane tempered glass windows, which are fire-resistant, and without question, fire-rated drywall.

List these items for the agent and demand a lower premium. You will not lose since your house will not burn down. During a major area fire, the other homes will burn down but yours will stand. No guarantees, but with aforementioned innovations, this author feels your house will have a better than 90% chance of survival. It will take a blow torch to burn down your home.

The best odds to win in a casino, if you are a good player, is 42%. The chance your house will burn down if properly constructed is 1%. Beat the odds. (See segment on Landscape Fire Prevention.) This is a good time to share with friends and neighbors. Oh, and put the insurance deductible in a savings account. It will double with the interest before you ever use it. A 99% chance. Good odds!

Nothing in this book are simple suggestions. They are a path to your better way of life.

STYLE OF HOMES

Beautiful and Alluring

Renowned architects have preferences to the style of homes they design. Frank Lloyd Wright designed only art deco homes, as did Richard Neutra. Paul Revere Williams designed larger traditional houses. Their homes are showcases today. These are 20th century architects who had innovative ideas formed by lots of engineering to fit their plans.

One century prior, these homes could not have been constructed since there was no engineering to support such exotic structures. Today, these homes cannot be remodeled. They can be refurbished but not changed since these architect's homes are historically preserved. The city for which they were built keeps them intact as "Heritage Homes."

The same can be said of the Romans who built structures not to be altered through time. Prior to the Roman Empire, homes were dealt with as the homeowners desired. That is where you come in.

You can build what you want as long as it is in keeping with the street and neighborhood. When it comes down to resale, you want top dollar to recoup plus profit for all your sweat and anguish.

The most popular style of house to emerge in the last 20th century was the bungalow. You can say the bungalow was a traditional home since so many were built at a time. This is called a development, tract homes, or a subdivision.

The bungalow homes were everywhere in this country. If you owned a bungalow, you were in the middle class. Ironic as it is, the homeowner never associated their home with the term "bungalow" since it originated in Europe and the Far East. The garage was for one car, since homeowners at the time had only one automobile. All homes had redwood siding, wood shingles, single-pane glass windows, no insulation, a tank water heater, a thirty-amp electrical panel, floor furnace, no air conditioning, toggle switches, and composition roofing. Sometimes gravel or rock roofing.

The bungalow is a one-story cottage first introduced about 500 AD in Spain. Prior to this time, houses were built one-story with one room. The bungalow added privacy by building interior walls. But it took 1,000 years for this concept to take hold in Europe. About the year 1,500, France with activist objection, designed and built bungalows throughout the country. Other countries followed suit and the bungalow became the desired house in which to live.

Not until after the war was the bungalow a must-have in America. Developments, starting in New York, sprang up throughout the nation but with added amenities. The bedrooms were separated from the general living area with interior walls, private bathrooms, and a separate kitchen. These homes had something in common. They all had a one-car garage in the rear yard with long driveways from the street or sometimes an alley. No two-car garages, but some had an oversized one-car space that had other uses, such as storage and laundry facilities, which came a decade later.

The bungalows had redwood siding in common. Redwood was chosen for its durability since the architects would bet their bottom dollar these bungalows were to last far into the future since they were the first-ever complete living structure.

Let's give these architects credit, even if the bungalow did not last probably their lifetime. The concept lives on in the form of condominiums with a two-car garage. Living in a bungalow in this country puts America in the forefront when it came to the preferable lifestyle. Most could not conceive of a better one. Then came the ranch-style home.

In 1950, the city fathers approved larger subdivided lots. This author wonders why, when some cities come up with something good, other cities don't accept it? But this time, other cities took hold. They approved wider lots to accommodate wider homes. This approach led to the ranch homes. The frontage was wider to accommodate a garage in the front, leaving the rear yard landscape to be larger, and made room for a pool. Now, homeowners could put their autos in one garage.

Many of you never heard the words, "Move your car, I need to get out." The ranch home was a huge boost to property values. They cost more, but resold for a lot more.

Then along came the contemporary house. The contemporary house designed by Frank Lloyd Wright and Richard Neutra had clean lines with minimum mouldings and minimum exterior wall décor except for masonry.

Today, contemporary homes called "modern" are everywhere, especially in the desert and beach regions but not many in suburban areas. Contemporary homes are nice to visit, but not that nice in which to live. Glass walls are beautiful to see out from, but others can see in!

Also, there is the comfort factor. Open space and seating is not that desirable. As stunning as a contemporary home is, it has yet to overcome the warmth and look of having wall space—and because of this, not many contemporary homes have been built in the last century.

It's not the style of house that makes it modern, it's the makeup of the house through and through. It can be ranch, bungalow, French, English, or contemporary. This book covers every aspect of what should be addressed in every square inch of the modern house. Beautiful and alluring. Like a moth attracted to a flame.

The middle class brought bungalows for $900.00 in 1920 and sold them for $10,000 in 1950. These homes were luxurious living for almost one century. Today, a bungalow in Los Angeles sells for $400,000. As wonderful as the bungalow was, it is going the way of the dinosaur.

The author's parents bought a bungalow in 1954 for $11,500 and the estate sold it for $450,000 in 2005. In 1967, this author's mother had a mortgage-burning ceremony, which was a gallant event. The house was paid in full. Unfortunately, this author cannot say the same. Why does this author need money for writing this book after receiving such an inheritance? Because proceeds had to be split six ways. Bottom line is you need to get your friends (future remodelers) to buy this book!

The bungalow is no longer built today but many thousands still stand all over the country. They stand to be remodeled and expanded with additional rooms. Some have been torn down and replaced by larger two-story houses.

Today, bungalows are no longer built by developers. Home-owners demanded more. They want a large kitchen to accommodate available appliances. The bungalow is considered traditional.

Ranch-Style Homes

The first transformation started in Memphis, Tennessee when the ranch-style home was introduced. This meant wider lots became available with the sprawling landscape. Quickly, California adopted this type of structure and it took hold immediately as a ranch house, but without the ranch.

Ranch-style homes were an expansion of the bungalow. The basic difference was the garage. The ranch-style home placed the garage in the front with a "U" shape driveway in some cases.

The middle class were forging ahead. Next came a two-story house with garages in front. This was no longer considered a ranch, but an innovation of multiple types of architecture.

Two-story houses hold two major advantages: one is the house can be larger on a smaller lot and costs less to build per square foot of livable space, but the garage costs more since the room above requires additional load bearing. The second story adds to a larger investment providing the most "bang for the buck." It costs a lot to build but it will bring the best resale value.

One and two-story homes have endured the last century. The style of homes have not changed appreciably. There is the French Classic, the French Mansard, English Tudor, Traditional Classic, Contemporary and the Mediterranean. What style to choose? That's easy—whatever is most common on your street and in your neighborhood. You cannot build a Mediterranean-style house in the Ascaya section in Las Vegas but you can do it on your street if it fits the common style in the neighborhood.

Bottom line: what style is a good fit for the future? Is it traditional exterior and contemporary (clean lines) interior? Period!

As aforementioned, the best way to go for resale from this day forward is a traditional home with a contemporary interior. Look to the future, pure and simple.

TIPS ON BUYING A HOME

If you have no choice in buying a house, such as from a family trust, or the house if the only one available near your desired school district, then do so. But if you have a choice, first and foremost, look for the most inexpensive house on a good street. This will allow you to remodel extensively and not lose any of your remodeling investment (if you do it right).

Sometimes there is more than one home of the same size on the market. Which one to choose? The number one consideration is if the backyard faces north. This is also good Feng Shui. A Feng Shui proper house is desired by many, not just the Chinese. You may not believe in Feng Shui, but this author believes in the axiom, "Don't take a chance." You may or may not sell to Chinese buyers, but Feng Shui has a humongous resale value to everyone.

When the backyard faces north, this adds tremendous value because early morning sun and evening sun do not shine directly into your house. Planting becomes so much easier for most gardens and requires less watering. Drought-tolerant plants are not necessary and weeding is at a minimum.

How many potential home buyers ask the Realtor about the north direction? According to Coldwell Banker, none. If the sun shines in, then a covered patio will be a consideration. The pool will still have sun coming in from the east and west but not the south, which means the pool will not have sunlight all day.

The Cul-De-Sac

If there is a house available at the end of a cul-de-sac, it generally costs less. Most buyers don't know why. It's because of the automobiles as they turn, shining their headlights into this house.

The average cul-de-sac house sells for 20% less. If you buy one, then every dollar you spend remodeling will bring you 20% less. Food for thought.

But with that said, a house on a cul-de-sac or dead end street is safe. Any police department will verify that burglaries occur less on such streets. The sophisticated burglar wants and escape route. One way in and one way out is not suitable. They scratch these homes as targets. Some cities do not have cul-de-sac streets, such as Chicago. Best to buy any house on a cul-de-sac street except those on the turn-around.

Lot Coverage

Lot coverage is a very important item to be addressed. If the house takes up so much of the property that the planning department will not allow expansion, before making an offer you must confer with the appropriate authorities on how much you can expand. If it looks like it's not much and the department concurs, then pass.

Be proactive not inactive. Go to the departments with your potential purchase and get upfront advice. You will be surprised how accommodating they will be for you. Take with you pictures of the house and lot, both front and rear. Ask if there are prohibitions and what the maximum is that you can expand. Ask about where you cannot put fences and walls and the height restrictions, if any. Also ask about decks and balconies. You cannot ask too many questions.

Don't be caught in the dilemma of not being able to expand. You may be looking at a property with slopes. Sloping up or sloping down. This is called a "hillside" lot. These lots are more common since 1950 when lots started being built on hillsides—but only build so far to the hill.

If the lot is sloping up, there is a good chance you will have a backyard. In this case, a house facing north may not come into play. Construction downhill will require additional engineering due to the possibility of the soil moving. Homeowners opt for decks to replace the backyard lawn. This upside for you is that most downhill lots have a good view. This adds to the resale value. Let's be realistic: a lot with a view and no backyard is worth less. Take that into consideration when making an offer, especially if you have small children.

A lot sloping up has limited possibilities. You can only realistically build so far to the hill. This limits the size of your house but gives you one big advantage over the down sloping lots. You have a backyard—generally it is a minimum of fifteen feet. You may have to put in a retaining wall to hold back some of the hill but you have a yard, albeit smaller than a level lot. Downside is, sometimes with little or no view.

What is the tradeoff? Upside with no view or downside with a view? The answer is an even 50/50 unless the down slope also has a view. Up sloping lots have more cars parked on the street. See for yourself when looking at a future purchase.

Okay, so you read this far and you don't have in mind such streets since you have open land. But some of the aforementioned facing the north still comes into play: The farm house, orchard property or a wine country home, if you can afford it, should also observe the same planning as any other house but it may infringe on upper class property. That is another subject!

BUILDING CODES

Building codes vary from state to state and country to county but what is common universally is that you must follow them. The codes are usually initiated by the state and city councils leaving the building departments to enforce them. If you are not happy with code requirements, don't blame the plan checkers. They are simply enforcing the rules, as required.

One county or state may have different requirements and the state has imposed requirements that the building departments have not yet implemented. Also, there are codes the city doesn't want to enforce. As an example, the state may require all doors to be 32" wide but the city may allow 30" wide room doors due to constrain on spaces, especially in older and/or smaller homes.

There are some requirements set down by the state that are a "must" to follow. These are related to fire protection and energy efficiency. Soon, there will not be anywhere in the country where you can purchase non-efficient toilets and faucets. Home Depot stopped selling these water guzzling items in 2012.

In addition to building codes, there are planning and zoning codes, energy codes and fire codes. County departments may have their own rules to follow, which are not part of state requirements. Your house may be situated in a high-rated fire zone therefore, you have more stringent requirements. The most pertinent code requirements are lot coverage, house location on the lot, and setbacks. These particular county rules are open to a variance or modification. The county or city, in some cases, charge a hefty fee to the homeowner to argue against all or part of these rules. It is the job of the planning commissioners to make a determination by denying outright, complete approval or conditional approval.

If you are determined to fight for your modification to a code, you must be prepared. Showing up at the hearing and simply asking for approval will seldom make a difference. You must be prepared. First, determine the required fees for your request. Follow the guidelines and hire someone to present your case with conviction. A lawyer can do this but there are also many professionals who do this job full time. What are their fees? You need architectural plans to present at the meeting. What are their fees?

Do your homework. Research other properties that have received such approval. It is also helpful to invite your neighbors to stand up for you and your project.

Not all rules require a major fight. Some may only require a meeting in an office with a planner or a desk clerk. You still need to pay the fees but they will be a lot less. Have architectural plans anyway to support your case and get the best representation you can afford. With all this in place, you have a good chance to get your approval.

If you get denied, it does not have to end there. You can appeal it to the higher administration, such as the city council. Start everything over again and add much bullets to the presentation.

Here is an example: You have an equestrian property but your lot does not fit the guidelines for stables and horses, but it comes close. That's where the research comes in. Find other properties nearby that have the same existing situation. It is not important that they were there prior to the new law or got approval like you desire.

If you follow these guidelines and get approved, send a note to this author and celebrate approval. Celebrate getting the permit and celebrate final inspection. If you want what you want, then make your presentation the best of the best.

THE UPPER CLASS

Who are the upper class? How are their names different than yours and mine? Answer: unlimited funds. Some say the upper class is 6% of the American population. They say this 6% controls 80% of the globe.

Who are the upper class? They are not lottery winners who win millions on one ticket. They are not the athletes who earn huge sums for their athletic abilities. They are not the celebrities who earn a great deal of money performing. They are not the innovators or inventors who get lots of money in return for their accomplishments.

So how do you define the upper class in this time and age? It's cut and dry. Today, if one person earns a million dollars per year, continually from this day forward, they are in the upper class. Included are their heirs. If one makes a million, that's great but if one makes a million, per year, for the rest of their lives, then they enter the upper class.

So the upper class status will never be reached by us, so what? Who cares? Well it would be nice! That doesn't mean we cannot live in a great house. We may not have a 1,500 square foot media center or maybe no media center at all but we can create a well—designed home on a much smaller scale and it will be just fine.

Let us build or remodel the best we can and live and let live. Start with the best plan and add amenities as your budget warrants. Keep in mind that we are living in the Golden Age of America. Take advantage of your abilities and your aspirations. You can survive! After all, how much land does one man need?

There is a story about greed during the time of the early settlers. Those who wanted land were asked to participate in a land grabbing day sponsored by the township. Participants were lined up and told to run as far as they could and return by sunset. The land they covered would be theirs to keep. One participant ran and ran. When he got as far as he could go, he pushed himself even further then returned, running as fast as he could to return to the finish before sunset. A few feet short, in total exhaustion, he collapsed and died. How much land does a man want?

Greed is the backbone of America. The railroad, steel, and oil industries are filled with cases of greed—which transformed to fortitude, luck, and perseverance.

These enterprises are no longer available to the entrepreneur. Today it is the Silicon Valley. Tomorrow it will be holograms. We will most likely be part of this phenomenon.

Why care? If we live in a comfortable home, drive a nice car and take occasional sea cruises, then what else does a man want?

Think of it this way: you walk outside with a bottle of drinking water and look up at the sun. This is the same sun that shone down on your grandparents, all the presidents of the United States, Jesus, and Mohammed. Take a drink of water. This is the same recycled water which has been on earth for millions of years.

Richard Kim went to Vegas and won 3.5 million dollars playing baccarat in the casino. He kept returning for more and finally lost everything. How much land does a man want?

PERMIT PROCESS

Yogi Berra said, "If you come to a fork in the road, take it." Fortunately, you don't have to guess as there is a permit process in this country. This is what makes America great. The guidelines you must follow are why houses are built better every year. The requirements for permits is what makes our homes safer, energy efficient, strong, and longer lasting than ever, and anywhere else on the globe.

Ordinances, in many cases, have been enacted as a result of devastation from disasters. When there are earthquakes, engineers change designs and require better standards to withstand future earthquakes. If the earthquake is right under your house, your house has no chance. But in the past, buildings near earthquakes also crumbled and some, more devastatingly than others.

Upgrades will not make your house earthquake-proof, but it can become earthquake resistant. With that said, bungalows built after the war had wood siding, small foundations (30% of today's requirements), and no engineering, and they withstood all earthquakes because they shifted and did not crumble.

After major fires where buildings burnt to the ground, fire codes were enacted for all new construction: from fire retardant roofing to fire retardant drywall, from cement board siding to stucco, and the elimination of spark intrusion, even vents.

After a major flood, houses were required to build higher above ground and overhead electrical wiring to the houses was required to be buried with cabled lines under the house.

Generators will soon be required in all flood area homes unless the feeding wires are underground. Sewers, which flow directly into the street trunk line, must have backup devices to prevent the neighbors' sewer from flowing into your home.

After a drought, water conservation plumbing fixtures and low flow faucets to sprinkler heads became a requirement in hot climate zones. Now they are required elsewhere in the country.

ENERGY SAVING SOLUTIONS

Not all requirements follow a disaster. Energy savings are a very big factor for many, especially in extreme weather conditions. Whenever possible, build on a concrete slab floor. Concrete slab floors make the house stronger, energy efficient, and keep furry animals out.

Even if you have an existing raised floor, build your addition on a concrete slab. That's the best you can do. Since many of us grew up in homes with raised floors, concrete floors seem harder to walk on. But consider that tile floors will crack more easily if laid on wood floor construction. To avoid cracking, the floor laymen put cement over the wood when laying tile. On slab floors, there is no need for a cement layer. Hardwood floors are warmer on wood construction, but now a layer of rubber matting over the concrete gives the hardwood floor insulation and comfort to walk on.

As aforementioned, concrete slabs are used in nearly all new construction except where the floor is raised substantially in flood areas. Every commercial building is on a concrete floor no matter how many stories high.

Another way to save on energy is to caulk around doors and window openings in the insulation stage. This, along with wall and ceiling insulation, will cut your energy bill down a minimum of 20%, which pays for itself in a short period of time.

The next best (but very important) energy saver is installing double-pane glass doors and windows. They are also good for security as they are more difficult for intruders to break. They almost need a sledge hammer that would make lots of noise. So if you see someone casing homes on your street with a sledge hammer in hand, lock your gates.

Garage doors come insulated but are not generally required although insulated garage sectional doors are quieter.

There is no question that LED lighting is the way to go. Every built-in light should be LED as the savings are immense. Although LED lighting is not required everywhere, it will be soon. Be ahead of the game.

Okay, so you have lived in your house for a zillion years without a disaster. Why should you be stuck with the costs of these permit requirements? Number one is resale. Number two is the cost of homeowner's insurance. (Be prepared for the tax assessor to raise the value of your home, which triggers the insurance underwriter to raise your premium.)

You show the homeowners insurance agent all the items now in your home to prevent loss from a disaster to obtain a lower premium. Also in your letter, draw pictures of how you removed large trees touching your house in the event that the tree touching your house is a protected tree by the department, then fight to get permission to remove it. Fight, fight, fight. As part of this, there is no way for burning embers to get into your attic—they will be receptive.

Positively, these items are expensive but if everyone must adhere, it makes the building more valuable. A new house and a house retrofitted with these amenities will bring a higher appraised value than the older house on your block of the same footage.

Unfortunately, you will be doing things to your house that will not be a part of the aforementioned disasters, especially drought. There is not much one can do to prevent hurricanes, tornados, fires or floods from occurring. Protect against them but they will come!

What do you do? As more of these catastrophes occur, the stricter the building code requirements will become. Be assured protection from all will be addressed. How long will it take? There is no set date but a good guess is when a huge spaceship capable of carrying many people will set off to colonize another planet in our far-off galaxy. But that's then. What about now?

One disaster that can be overcome is drought. Unfortunately, drought has not been addressed properly. When it rains, a billion gallons of water each day flows into the ocean or percolates into the soil. Can we not harvest this water? Yes, it would be expensive, but what are taxes for? Wherever possible, desalination should be implemented.

We need roads and bridges for travel, but we need water to survive. The water we have today is the same water that's been on earth for a billion years. Harvest the water and move on to the prevention of hurricanes and tornados causing power outages. In this day and time we can harvest water and do away with power outages.

In 2017, Puerto Rico suffered a 90% power outage due to a hurricane. We can't prevent hurricanes but we definitely can prevent power failures.

This author has power lines running to the rear of his property. Two blocks away, there are no visible power poles since they are underground. Strong underground lines are the future. New developments in this country require underground lines. The answer is to retrofit the power lines on all streets in this country and Puerto Rico, eliminating the danger and inconvenience avoiding the missed viewing of the closing minutes of a close football game. Don't want to see and hear, "The winner is…" and the power goes out?

The building inspector is called to come out to your site. Notes, notes, notes. Is there one building inspector who reads the notes? Unfortunately, not one. Why? Because the notes are too general.

Notes are put on plans to satisfy the permit agency, which satisfies the county above, as the state requirements are mandated to the county. There is generally not enough time allotted to the inspector to review everything on the plans. Therefore, unfortunately, items are missed as more and more notes are on the plans and it is difficult for the inspectors to do their job efficiently.

What's the answer? Very simply, have a checklist for the inspector to follow. Now the inspector arrives with only the permit copies.

Unfortunately, there is favoritism. Some plan checkers favor some architects over others. You can say it is a way of life. But you don't want to be caught in this dilemma. What do you do?

Research what other permits have been issued and check them out. Why are you required to do this when so and so did not? Answer: favoritism.

Unfortunately, favoritism is widespread in this industry from political favoritism to friends and relatives. You want to be on a level playing field. Check out why items are requested. Call them out if you can show your requirements are not warranted. Additionally, architects and engineers sometimes over design. Areas to watch for are roof structures, bearing beams, foundations oversized, more steel and attachments than are required. If your project is large enough, take your plans to another engineer for a second opinion. You get a second opinion for a heart transplant; why not for your engineering—it's your money.

Don't Blame the Inspector

With all this said, homes are built better and better every year and more energy efficient. We need to change from thinking of ourselves as unfortunate to fortunate.

You will pay a plan check fee and a permit fee and fees for this and fees for that. You must pay all these fees if you want a permit. They are holding you hostage. Can't say these departments are correct but we all can agree they are greedy.

During the entire process of remodeling, the homeowner, contractor and architect have two things in mind: they relish the gratification of getting the plans stamped with approval and passing the final inspection. Forty years ago, three sheets of plans were required for most major remodeling projects. Today, the average set of plans is about fifteen sheets and the sheets are twice the size. The plans had white lines on blue paper, thus, the name "blue prints."

These days, the average homeowner is not able to decipher what everything is on the plans. Forty years ago, most inspectors came from the building industry as former contractors. That still holds true today but the majority of inspectors come from college educated engineers and many have never pounded a nail. If a person gets a degree in engineering, becomes a contractor and later, a building inspector, the job will not last long. They will be called up to be a senior inspector and given an office desk.

Forty years ago, a person wanting to be an inspector took a test for one of four inspections: electrical, plumbing, mechanical (heating) and general building. Most were former contractors in their prescribed trade of expertise. The four inspectors visited the site and gave approvals if all was done properly. This is still done today, primarily for commercial buildings.

But things rapidly changed to one inspector to approve the entire project. This reduced inspection time from weeks to a few days. Today, in order for the inspectors to be proficient, they attend numerous in-house meetings to keep up with the ever-changing codes. During the 1920 construction boom, the building codes read 1,386 words. Today, the New York City building code reads 265,850 words.

Don't blame the inspector if a correction is left for you to fix. Inspectors routinely sit in on code changes and requirements set down by the elected officials. They are there to enforce the rules. If a traffic cop stops you for a misdemeanor offense, he is not doing it for their personal observation, but for the rules they are required to enforce. So is the building inspector. They have to make observations as they are required.

INSPECTIONS: WHAT TO EXPECT

Inspectors are accommodating. They will be as helpful as the rules allow. They will give helpful advice. Again, they may be former contractors so they know your pain.

Some homeowners believe that getting a permit is a losing proposition. Not so. A permit and inspection are insurance that the job is done right. Why would you want to do an addition or a kitchen remodel without inspection to ensure your house is done properly? The inspection adds value to your house, which transfers to money in your pocket. Additionally, an inspection culminating in a final approval, is a great asset for resale.

Many officials require engineering inspection prior to building inspection. This means the engineer of record (the one who engineered the original project) is to inspect the forms and steel placement that was designed for the permit. This observation report is left on the site for the inspector. This alleviates the inspector having to check the steel placement, trenching depth, and framing structure. It is necessary for the inspector to verify the forms are properly laid out to the required setbacks (which is the required distance between the proposed structures to the property lines).

It works this way: The engineer does the computation for building approval. Plans with engineering are approved. The engineer of record inspects the phases and gives a report. When the inspector arrives on the site and sees the report, the project will proceed to the next stage, provided other requirements for the plans are met. This method is meant to ensure the structural integrity of your house, not found in third world countries. This author has a comment about this lack of sequence: corrupt!

The inspector signs a card, which is on the site along with the stamped approved plans. First, the inspector checks to see the affidavit by the engineer signed his approval with the plans. Then the following inspections are made as work is done. First the layout of the trenches as per the plan. Then the floor joist or slab with the underground plumbing and the framing, including roof nailing. This inspection is relatively new since sheathing plywood is used instead of 1 x 6 spaced sheathing formerly used for wood shingles (no longer approved due to instability). Then plumbing, electrical and heating ducts (known as rough inspection), lathing if stucco is used, sometimes cement applied around showers, insulation, and drywall nailing.

Some inspections are done simultaneously, therefore, not as many return trips unless there are corrections. There are two possible corrections: substandard, misplaced or missing items, such as not enough slop on the sewer line or not enough protection for electrical wires fed through the studs. Second and much more serious is the dreaded correction. If you deviate from the plans, you will be caught at this time. The inspector simply will say to take the plans in and have them revised to reflect your change and then walk away to the coffee shop.

You can be proactive. Have modified changes approved before you call for inspection. When an inspector is due to come to the job site, there are two things you must know. First, do not talk to the inspector. Do not even discuss the time of day. Be sure every person on site also knows to keep their mouth shut tight.

While engaging in casual conversation, the inspector will have time to find something small to delay the project. Stay clear. You are looking for one thing and one thing only—a signature of approval to continue working.

The second is do not argue or question the notice of "non-approval." Never complain to the superiors. This will antagonize and cause you untold headaches. If it's a major correction, have your architect deal with it by taking the correction to the department and requesting how to fix it. Be cordial at all times. It will go a long way.

There are no other progress inspections after the drywall nailing inspection. The last inspection is final.

Prior to final, you can move in. There is no longer an occupancy approval. You can move in while awaiting the final approval. Some cities require the planning and fire departments come out and bless the project. Generally, these are only to see you have complied. Most times, no worries.

Sometimes, homeowners will not call for final inspection. Bad idea. The permit time will lapse and when it's time to sell or refinance, the closing of the sale will stop cold. You return to the department to get the final but…no way, Jose. You must pay a penalty and the permit fee charged at the time. Additionally, if some code changes have been invoked, then you may have to make these changes, too, to comply. Money out the window not to mention time lost for your refinance or sale.

Be prepared for the final inspection. All exterior and interior to be primed with at least one coat of paint, all light fixtures to be in place and all electrical items to have cover plates, all plumbing fixtures working properly and exhaust fans working, fireplace glass doors, tile properly set around fireplaces (6-inch sides, 12-inch top and 18-inch hearth, to be tile or stone or equal), shower doors or shower curtain in place, roof vents according to plans, driveway paved to the street, all debris removed from the premises, and house number visible from the street.

Generally the inspector will not be concerned about fences and landscape unless they are on the plans. If you have a pool, that will be addresses under a separate permit and another inspection or the general inspectors. Entire pool area to be fenced five feet high or four feet nearer the pool. Gates must swing out and self-latch, some departments require exterior doors of your house leading to the pool area to be alarmed for child safety.

In the event that you have a required septic system, then the approval must accompany the plans for final inspection.

If you are not sure that you have everything covered, call for final inspection anyway. You will find the inspector to be accommodating and will help you get through the process. After all, inspectors also remodeled their homes.

RESALE

Getting the Returns You Want

Few people, if any, remodeled their houses for resale. The objective is to get what they want, not thinking of what another family desires in their house. This means a better kitchen and family room in most cases. But in the long run, it goes much further. Remodeling your house for you to live in is commendable but what about the future? First and foremost, you want the best for your children. You want to put them in their own bedroom and have access to your nice kitchen and family room. This is a given.

Children assimilate to what is in the house, they accept what is there. A good layout of your house does not register with them. They accept all conditions. Children do not have an inkling of what can be better for them. You should not be pulled into that sphere.

What is acceptable or convenient is not always correct. Tandem bedrooms may be acceptable but is a killer for resale unless the new owner uses them for a nursery or a private study or office. You want to avoid killer items. They are deadly! The appraiser knows!

So you remodel your house for you and not someone else. What happens if your job requires you move away so you must sell, or someone happens to knock on your door and wants to give you more than the house is worth?

Eminent domain displaced thousands of homes and will continue as highway and parks are necessary for this expanding country. If this time comes, you want the most for your home. So the unplanned happens. Will you be ready?

Your house will go through the appraisal process. If your house is better than your neighbors' then you will get more even if your neighbors have the same size house on the same size lot. You must move and have to go through the appraisal process. Be prepared for that day.

APPRAISAL

Prepare for the Appraiser

Get ready for the appraiser. The exterior yards should be immaculate, not even a leaf showing on the ground. Everything you had been putting off doing for your yard, such as fixing the fence or getting new trash cans, do it now.

The interior is to be as nice and neat as you can afford. Clean all windows and mirrors, leave no ashes in the fireplace. Polish the floors and clean the tile grout. Clean the garage. Make your interior and exterior look like it was just built.

Come appraiser day, be sure there are no boxes containing your stuff showing anywhere. Put a color plant or two in every room. Just before the appraiser comes, turn on all the lights inside and outside of your home, even if it is daytime. Appraisers know these tricks. When they see you have prepared, they will assume you are looking for the highest possible appraisal. Details are the difference between ordinary and extraordinary.

Real estate companies can be helpful. A good Realtor will appraise your house, no charge. This is a good way to go since their appraisal will help you know approximately what your house will sell for. They do this hoping they will eventually get your listing. Chances are, you will absolutely consider this Realtor. If the time comes to sell and you have adhered to everything in this book, you will get the best return.

Consider one significant factor. You have remodeled and know the ropes. If you sell then you take the knowledge with you to begin the process all over again for your new house. You were at the command of others; now you will be in command.

Golden Age

We are now living in the Golden Age of America. It began in the 1860s with iron ore converted to steel. Steel, stronger than anything else at the time, remains the backbone of our buildings and bridges. Without steel, our buildings would crumble as they did after the Roman Age. Steel used extensively for railroad tracks kept the veins of America flowing.

The period of our Golden Age was not that long age in terms of humanity on earth. There were Golden Ages throughout time. The Greek philosopher Hesiod introduced the term in his *Works and Days* when referring to the period when the Golden Race of man lived. The Golden Ages, mankind's inhabitance on earth, started with the advent of something big and ended with a war, in most cases.

America's Golden Age has transcended wars. It is as if they did not happen. An analogy would be the coach of Alabama who led his team to national prominence. Woody Hayes would yell at a player for what he did wrong. Instead of giving up and walking off the field, he went back in there and played his heart out for the coach. That is America to you. Get 100,000 soldiers to die for this country and through the tears, move on as Voltaire said, press on to greater achievements of the future.

So you thought this book was about home remodeling and not philosophy? A well-built house has a well-built foundation.

What is ahead in this Golden Age? What to expect tomorrow and when will it end? The last thing first—it will end! How long it will last is directly related to the time when men become violent and greedy. As with all previous dynasties that ended after the overthrow of the violent and greedy. There is a good chance it will not happen while you are living in this Golden Age.

With the advent of steel and its potential came the ingenuity of American minds. What can be next? Who can stop an educated engineer, free to think outside the box?

Then along came electricity. Electricity was invented by Thomas Edison but the American engineers put the phenomenon to work. At the same time came the gas-powered automobile. In less than 150 years, this country embedded itself in the Golden Age.

The housing industry followed suit. Homes are bigger and better—or they will get that way by following the strict guidelines in this book.

Then along came the telephone. This convenience made the housewife feel secure. To be readily in touch with their families and friends made life less burdensome. In this Golden Age, life became ever so happy.

Then came television. The homeowner connected for the first time with the outside world.

Then along came the cell phone, thanks to the American engineers upgrading your lifestyle ever better every day.

But when will this Golden Age end? Not during our lifetime. It can go on for hundreds of years or until our form of government changes. Do you think this could be possible?

China went from imperialism to communism to capitalism or semi-capitalism. China's era is about to change again. China, postwar, was limited to couples having only one child due to foreseeable over population. It worked. The population slowed and those many children entering the labor force allowed for low paying jobs. Thus, China had the lowest costs of production. These children are older now and retiring. Where are the children to continue the "Made in China" syndrome? There are none. The government is heading for a new era and it will not be golden.

What's in store for our housing industry? No one knows for sure but based upon innovation to date, the author will speculate: Garages will be built to accommodate four cars in a two-car garage space. Front door knobs will be programmed for owners to enter without a key. The kitchen appliances will be various colors of stainless steel but mostly black. Roofs will be constructed with solar tiles and be rodent-proof, flooring will be warmer to walk on. Windows and exterior doors will be shatter-proof, showers will be digital, toilets will be paperless, weeds will be eradicated with granules, lighting will be without fixtures, cabinet doors will open with a touch, doors and walls will be completely soundproof and windows and door glass will be shatterproof.

What about the country's future? We have ingrained in our American life, the freedom of expression. This leads directly to innovation. The freedom to perform without restrictions. This is called "the runaway train."

This author plans to write a book on the "runaway train." Would you read it?

What is good today is better tomorrow. In 1960, the TV series "Dick Tracey," detective Tracey had a wrist band that he could talk into at the bureau. Today we can converse with the world using a smartwatch. Who knew?

Communication to the outside from all areas of the house, hot water upon demand, living rooms will be eliminated, dining rooms will be smaller but expandable, and there will be two office rooms.

Probably the biggest achievement will be homes constructed of steel rather than lumber. Steel studs and steel rafters. The house of the future will be almost fireproof. Bamboo cabinets everywhere.

Go with the punches. Do your thing and let bygones be bygones. You are doing your part by improving the middle class home. Stay smart!

HOUSES OF THE FUTURE

Know What the Future Will Bring

In June 1957, Disneyland introduced the House of the Future in Tomorrowland. It was a contemporary style suspended room with a center/common foyer. The author toured this house during every visit to Disneyland. Everyone thought it was virtually looking into the future to the year 1986. Never happened!

The house designed and built by Monsanto Company and Michigan Institute of Technology was of fiberglass construction with lots of windows and designed for the middle class but it lacked furniture, had no garage, no yard at floor level, nor was there room for expansion.

The Monsanto building was removed in 1997. It was built sturdy but it was not for the American homeowner. No home of this prototype ever got built. The designers were missing one big item: livability.

Monsanto missed the mark. The best laid plans of mice and men missed the mark. But we are 100% sure what houses of the future were built from 1958 to this day because we are here. We know everything homeowners wanted we saw the finished product.

Monsanto called their house "futuristic." The futuristic house is not what someone envisions. No, it is the house that develops with time. You house! It's not the entire house that is futuristic; it's the items in the house. In 1957, televisions were 10" wide. Today they span the width of a football field.

Obviously, this holds true for any time in the past. Since ancient China, evolution in home living has changed and in 1957, the TV, in most cases, improved.

If you go back in time, any time, while knowing what the future will bring, you would wonder "Why do people not realize they can have a better life by instituting the future?"

All this is not close to being possible, but is it? The answer may be found in mathematics. When you add one number to another you get the sum. The key is the sum. You can add an array of numbers to get to the same sum.

Let's take the analogy to your home's fireplace. The fireplace is a fixture in your house. This fixture has been around since the beginning of civilization. No matter how it is designer or redesigned, it will only work with combustible energy: fire.

Will this fire change in the future? No. Inventing or suggesting a replacement for the fireplace will not happen. This holds true for the sinks, toilets, beds, entry doors, windows, and others, which are part of the past, present, and future.

Replacements for the necessities and luxuries will not happen in the future because they are the sum. No matter how you contort them, they will be the final foundation of your house. Looking into the future and making changes to this foundation will run you into a roadblock.

Back to mathematics. We've established that many different numbers added together will result in the same sum. There are many different fireplaces but one unit. The future cannot change the sum, it can only change the numbers.

A doorway has been built for two centuries at a height of 70 to 80." The height can be changed but the doorway will be there.

Using this data, what is the house of the future? Again, what Monsanto missed was the livability.

The house of the future is a place of comfort, convenience and security. Livable. The convenience of walking through the house from the front, rear doors, and garage without disturbing the rest of the house is achieved with halls, entrances to areas where family is not congregated for sleeping. Television will allow images to enter the room for entertainment and be life size.

The biggest innovation of the future will be a nuclear reactor to power your house. There will be no need for fossil fuel, solar or wind turbines. The reactor will be placed somewhere on the street and power all the nearby homes. Uranium the size of a fireplace log can power 100 homes for one year. Reactors will be on nearby planets before long. Stay tuned.

Security. Technology not bars on the windows. Technology ever advancing will provide exterior security. Door locks with easy openings will make your individual rooms secure.

Comfort. Beds will be ever more comfortable. Chairs and sofas will be such that you will not want to move.

Convenience. Cooking and laundry will be instant. Automatic waterless car wash in your garage. Instant hot water. Sprinklers robot controlled. Silent toilet flushing. Touch ID door locks, wireless electrical, shatterproof windows, and instant remote closing blinds.

Hygiene will be the concern of the homeowner. Kitchen and bath hygiene will be thoughtful items.

Exciting? Stick around.

THE HOMELESS

Get a Grasp

During the Dark Ages and before leprosy was common—a terrible disease. Lepers were outcasts, which is not different than today's homeless. No home and nowhere to live but on the streets. During the Golden Age, this issue must be addressed.

At the time that the author is writing this book, there are 215,000 homeless people in California alone. This is close to 1% of this country's population, and nearly 3% of the population of California—and the problem is growing.

There are two kinds of homeless: The ones who cannot make it in the real world, and those who want nothing other than to be left alone in their tents. This is going to be an ever-growing problem for this country because it is so easy to become homeless. No mortgage, no loans, and no responsibility. Just living day-to-day and looking for food to survive. It's very harsh to say, but that is the way all wild animals live. Why not live carefree? They will be satisfied to stay at the outskirts of town as did the lepers. Stop and think. No care in the world. "Why not indulge?" say the homeless. "The government will take care of us."

In cities such as Chicago, Boston, Los Angeles, San Francisco and New York, there is a solution. Put the homeless in temporary hotel rooms, or better yet, build smaller houses or a dormitory-style facility for them. Great! Altruistic. Build these and they will come. Why not come? Easy living off the taxpayers. Judges far and wide are demanding that city officials find solutions for the homeless, and find it now!

The worst example of a solution is by the Los Angeles mayor and city council. Each district was given a huge amount of money to come up with a solution or the money will go elsewhere. Every try driving on three wheels? Build it and they will come. A person evicted from their house would love a free place to stay. Wouldn't you?

At the current rate, California will have 300,000 homeless by 2025 if nothing is done. The same for Chicago, Boston, New York and many other cities.

Where does the money come from to take care of this increasing population? Answer: Off the backs of the lower class in the form of taxes. Money is needed for this endeavor. Sales tax and gasoline increases pay for these projects. No thought is given to the lower class. Working for a minimum wage, it takes an average of three to four hours of work just to pay for gas to get to and from work. When the lower class buys most anything for their convenience they pay a huge sales tax with a portion going to the homeless. They work to pay for someone else who is not working. This is not the American way.

Some lower class survive this dogma and find their way to the better life but the millions of these hard working Americans are carrying an albatross on their backs. In a majority of the cities of America sales tax has more than doubled in twenty years but wages have not. Gasoline taxes have increased ten-plus fold in thirty years.

Mike Pompeo, 2018 Secretary of State, once worked for $7.50 per hour. How much of this was taxed? Not much. But thirty-six years later, the wage is only double but the expenses of gas and sales tax have increased ten times.

There is an answer. It will come to you from this author. What I am about to tell you is worth the purchase of this book, alone.

First, what has this to do with you? Because, if you live on or near a street with homeless people, then it will substantially reduce the value of your house. Who would want to live there? Answer: If you are not homeless, no one.

Look to the Daily News in any city today. The lead story is typically an article about the homeless. It's everywhere in America today. You see pictures of the homeless trying to survive but it's what you don't see that stands out immensely. There are no Asians in the pictures. "Odd," you say? But let's explore.

The Asians are not there because they are not homeless. Where are they? With their families. Asian homes are built or remodeled to accommodate their parents. The family takes care of the elderly by adding facilities for them. The premise is simple. Take care of us when young and we will take care of you when you are old.

Records show that 80% of the homeless have families who know they are on the streets. If the families knew that a relative was on the street, they would intervene. Most likely take them in. At least give them comfort. The average family would do anything to get their loved ones off the streets.

Impossible task? Not in the slightest. It only takes a one-on-one conversation with the homeless person to ask about their family. Then a contact with this person is all it takes. It is surprising how much a homeless person can contribute to the household. How many homeless people have a family to turn to?

Bottom line: Hook up every homeless person with a family member. If the agencies would do this then there would be no homeless. The process is simple. Ask each homeless person if they have family. Then contact this family and ask if they will take this person in. How can it be more? If the Asians can do it 100% then you can do it 100%.

Some say the housing costs prevent the homeless from living in a house. Japan's housing costs more than the average American home and yet there are zero homeless on the streets. Elementary, my dear Watson!

CAREER IN CONSTRUCTION

Easy Way Out

During the years of the caveman, there was always work to be done in the dwelling. The cavemen hunted, protected their families, and worked in the cave. Floors had to be leveled, living sections had to be carved out, and ceiling heights were cut for convenience.

Joseph, the father of Jesus, was a construction worker. His trade was woodwork and carpentry. Today, these trades are millwork and farming. There has always been a demand for all types of experienced tradesmen from carpentry to plumbing and excavation to roofing. How to become experienced? Stay in the trade your entire working life.

From the days of the cavemen 'till today, there has always been work for the construction worker. Two things the building industry has to offer are a decent wage and the satisfaction of seeing one's accomplishments. Unlike other forms of employment, you can see your completed work for many years. How many workers looked at the Empire State Building and said, "I helped build that."

One drawback is that it is hard physical work, but it's as hard as you make it. One can put three shovels of dirt in a wheelbarrow in a minute or put in ten. The choice is yours. How hard do you want to work? Dale Nozothy, a roofer for forty-seven years, was asked "When are you going to retire?" He said, "When I stop enjoying the work." And roofing is the hardest of construction occupations.

This author got a job at age sixteen nailing plywood on a roof with a heavy construction hammer. The foreman wanted nine sheets nailed in one hour. After three days the job became rhythmical. That is when the unthinkable happened.

The contractor drove onto the site. He said to all the workmen standing around, "You're fired." He fired everyone except for the roof-nailer, me. I worked alone until the contractor got a new crew from the union pool. Moral of the story: Become a company person from *day one*. You signed up.

Moving on, Stepping Boldly

So you want to become a construction worker? You have various ways to start. From the top, buy a house and remodel it for resale (called flipping). Join the union as an apprentice. Union jobs are more difficult to come by and you need to pay dues. The upside is that the pay is good, but many times there is a lull in work time. You are put on a list and wait for the next opening.

Non-union work is steadier but pays less with little to no benefits. You can start as a non-union worker in residential and later join the union if you choose commercial. This author was lucky to get a job at sixteen-years-old. Those were enlightening years, meeting other workmen and talking about various projects. Union people are the greatest!

Learning architecture is a great benefit. As you rise in the work field, you need to read plans. Today, plans are complicated and will become more so. Doing your job per plans is a way to advance in this business. Also, to be mentioned are the directions that must be followed to do the job right.

Every college offers business classes. Take every class offered. If you cannot afford a university, attend a community college. Unfortunately, contractors worldwide think they know it all. They do not since improvements in technology and building change rapidly and they miss the boat.

Read periodicals in trade magazines, attend seminars and show up at trade shows. Every time you go, promise yourself to learn at least one new thing. Learn and keep learning. Be the best you can be.

So you want to be a contractor? Take the study course on both trade and legal laws. You will learn so much. Pass the test, become a contractor and continue the formation of this country.

But starting at the bottom and staying at the bottom is not how our country became great. On-the-job training is necessary and fulfilling except it keeps you at a lower level for a long time. You need education. Education is how our country became so great (among other things).

From the day you start work until the day you retire, you must educate yourself. This author, after so many years, is doing research for this book for you. It should never stop.

Take architecture in high school. Take all the shop classes that pertain to construction. Be committed 100%. It will pay off in the long run. Donald Trump studied in school while taking time to work on the job sites. He became president of the United States. Need I say more?

There is no other profession that can see one's accomplishments more than construction. The Empire State Building, built in only one year by Williams Corporation will live on in its legacy. Today with all the regulations, it takes one year to build a house.

You can go beyond the general contractor. Learn good design. A start would be to read this book. You need to visit large and small developments. Study what they are doing and incorporate these ideas into your portfolio.

While talking to a prospective client, tell them what you believe is good for them based upon your observances of an acceptable design that has been proven best for resale. Relay to the client that the best design is directly related to the value of their house. When you don't know about something, ask an expert.

REVERSE MORTGAGES

Start with an Agent

A reverse mortgage is not for everyone but it could be in time. Everyone should know about its potential. You or your spouse must be age sixty-two or older to have one. You might not be this age but perhaps your parents or grandparents are. This is a good way to live out your life than to have no mortgage payments. The interest is higher than current bank loans. Fees to get the loan are high but the qualifications are low.

More than 65% of homeowners cannot afford to buy the house they live in and 38% cannot even qualify for a loan of that amount. The down payment and the monthly payments are, most times, a real financial burden.

The way out is to sell your house and use the proceeds to buy another. Okay, that's what you will read in this book but what if you want to stay put? The reverse mortgage is the answer if your family members are sixty-two or older. The older someone is, the better their chances of qualifying. Sounds like capitalism? It is.

The process is long and arduous. Start with an agent. Agents have underwriters who set guidelines and determine your eligibility. If an agent determines you may qualify, you then sign papers.

You sign thirty-five pages of documents. You must pay about $150 for a home ownership counseling by phone so you know what you are getting into and understand the consequences. This is a phone interview. The government set up this rule for all reverse-mortgage loan companies to follow.

Next comes the appraisals. There are two. The first appraisal is to be paid by you. The second appraisal is paid by the underwriter

308

and is scheduled by them. You have no choice except you can dispute either appraisal if you wish to enhance your loan amount.

Prepare for the appraiser by getting your entire property in the best shape possible, putting on all the lights, both interior and exterior, even in the daytime. Clean up every area. The loan company will use the lower of the two appraisals as a guide to granting the amount for the loan.

You don't need to show substantial income, but you do have to disclose your ability to pay the property tax and homeowners insurance. No other requirement is necessary. This can come from your social security or pension if you are not working.

You must disclose your last three years of tax returns. The agent receives a good commission for this loan, therefore, they will assist you through this process. The agent's commission comes from the initial fees charged by the loan company, not from you. In addition to the interest, the loan company will add a small fee of about $30 to service the loan each month.

What are the benefits? Cash to you without making payments. Want to remodel your house? You will get money to do so without making payments if you qualify, and most do. More than 85% of eligible homeowners quality for a reverse mortgage.

Underwriters will make loans if your house is worth $300,000 or $3 million, or more. Upon closing the loan, you will receive a check to do whatever you want. This author suggests planting fruit trees. Plant the trees as soon as the loan closes.

Let's say you have read this book and decide to remodel. You use the reverse mortgage money and your savings. Then what? Refinance the reverse mortgage. Remember, the interest is higher but it is fixed for life as long as you live in your house for more than six months each year.

How can this be so easy? It's not! After you and your spouse's demise, your heirs must pay off the mortgage or sell the house. The big tax advantage is that the interest accrued over time can be deducted from taxes or proceeds if the house is sold. There will always be a positive balance since your house will inevitably go up in value over time. In fact, the increase in value is most times larger than the reverse mortgage payments. So you wonder, how do the loan companies come out?

First, they charge an upfront fee and you cannot refinance again for two to three years, which gives them a chance to make money on your loan interest and fees.

Bottom line: You have money to remodel in most cases. The mortgage company gets interest they recoup upon sale, and you don't have to make mortgage payments. Everyone wins but wins in comfort!

Additionally, you can make payments to reduce the loan balance. This will save money for your heirs, but—and it's a strong but—you cannot deduct interest payments on your tax returns unless you make these payments.

Want to be a reverse mortgage entrepreneur? Get a reverse mortgage and use the money to enlarge your house. Sell and buy a smaller house with a reverse mortgage. Okay, so you are older. But you can be active. It's like growing roses in the desert.

TIMES HAVE CHANGED SINCE MID-CENTURY

OUT	IN
Steel Framed Windows	Vinyl Framed Windows
Single-Panel Glass	Double Paned Glass
Tank Water Heaters	Tankless Water Heaters
70 Amp Electrical Services	100 Amp Electrical Services
Carpet Flooring	Hardwood or Tile Flooring
Natural Wood Hardwood Flooring	Composite Flooring
No Wall Insulation	Insulation Walls and Ceiling
Raised Conventional Floor Construction	Concrete Slab Floors
Large Living Rooms	Smaller or No Living Rooms
Hollow Core Doors	Solid Core Doors (for sound insulation)
Maximum Flow Faucets	Low Flow Faucets—Energy Efficient
Maximum Flush Toilets	Minimum Flow Toilets
Cast Iron Sewers	ABS Sewers
Galvanized Water Lines, Type in Copper	Copper Water Lines, Type L Copper
Cast Iron Sinks	Stainless Steel Sinks
White Appliances	Stainless Steel Appliances
No Door or Window Weather Stripping	All Weather Stripping

Eve Vents	Roof Vents
Wall Heaters	Whole House Heating (FAU)
Brick Fireplaces with Brick Chimneys	Pre-Fab Fireplaces with Frames/Stucco
Galley Kitchens	Kitchen Islands
Electrical Appliances	Gas Appliances, Electric Microwave
Plaster	Drywall
Toggle Wall Switches	Rocker Switches
Wood Siding	Cement Siding
Master Bath Wardrobe	Master Bath Walk-In Closet
Mortice Entry Locks	Bored Entry Locks
Non-Protected Wall Outlets	Safety Wall Outlets
Fluorescent or Incandescent Lights	LED Lights
Peek Hole Front Doors	Ring Manufactured Security
Asphalt Paving	Concrete or Stone Pavers
Shower Curtains or Framed Doors	Frameless Shower Doors w. Self-Cleaning Glass
Pictures Above Fireplaces	TV Above Fireplace
Floor Heaters and Ducts	Ceiling Heaters and Ducts
Tower Bars	Towel Racks
Cabinets with Exposed Hinges	Hidden Hinges
Cabinets with Frames	Frameless Cabinets

Tile Counters	Stone Counters
Large Tile Counter Backsplash	Small Tile Backsplash
Pantry with Painted Shelving	Non Sticking Shelves
Solar Panels	Solar Tiles
Mirrors Cemented on Wall	Picture Framed Mirrors
30" Height Bath Cabinets	34" Height Bath Cabinets Including Stone
Color Painted Ceilings/ Mouldings	White Ceilings/Mouldings (except natural wood finish)
White walls and Wallpaper	Color coordination walls (when book is being written). Colors are Black, White and Shades of Gray (see Chapter 7)
Bath Window for Ventilation	Ventilator Fans and Windows
Basement for Storage	Basement for Recreation and Storage
Laundry Machine Ringer	Washer with Agitator
Five Different Spoons	Seventeen Different Spoons
Redwood Siding	Fiber Cement Siding
Ivy Outside for Appearance	No Ivy (it attracts rats)
Doors with Curtains or Venetian Blinds	Doors with Adjustable Blinds Between the Glass

Wallpaper	Painted Wallpaper Directly on Walls
Landscape with Random Plants	Congruent Planting
Laundry Marching Ringer	No Ringer/ Washer Plate
Land Phones	Cell Phones
Local Police	Growling Dogs

BECOME A MILLIONAIRE, STEP BY STEP

Staying the Course

Bottom line, you cannot afford the space for this luxury, but at least you know the possibilities. Let's be pragmatic. Follow this author and design and build your house step by step. You will realize a very good profit if you sell. Then what? Start again!

Here is the bottom line. You have worked for minimum wage many years of your life or you sacrificed part of your living conditions. As you enter your mature years, you look back to what you have accomplished. You accomplished wage increases, an investment portfolio, but what about your real estate?

This paragraph is only for the strong at heart. Buy a house. Fix it up (using this author's methods), sell it, buy another and another until you can look back and pat yourself on the back for doing the best that can be done.

This author is also a pragmatic and after reading this book and agreeing with the content, you will go on your way. At least a map is drawn for you. Think about this. You find a map locating hidden treasure; you take a lifetime studying this map. Where does it lead you? To your house. Toughness!

A decade in your life goes by very fast. As you look back on a decade, you wonder what you have accomplished. Probably a lot, but what about the decade ahead? That's your challenge. Don't take a day or a year, take a decade. We may have eighty years in our lifetime but only seven or eight decades.

Plan for decades, not years. Plan for the future not the near future. Discover the opportunities. Staying the course has an impact on how good you will feel when it's all over. Want to wake up in your fabulous house? Then, without question, follow the guidelines in this book and create magic in your life!